T0353010

Angel
Intuition

About the Author

Tanya Carroll Richardson is a self-improvement/spiritual author, professional intuitive, and regular contributor to MindBodyGreen.com. Her other books include *Angel Insights*, *Zen Teen*, *Heaven on Earth*, and *Forever in My Heart: A Grief Journal*. Sign up for Tanya's free newsletter or follow her on social media by visiting tanyarichardson.com.

To Write to the Author

If you wish to contact the author or would like more information about this book, please write to the author in care of Llewellyn Worldwide, and we will forward your request. Llewellyn Worldwide cannot guarantee that every letter written to the author can be answered, but all will be forwarded. Please write to:

Tanya Carroll Richardson
℅ Llewellyn Worldwide
2143 Wooddale Drive
Woodbury, MN 55125-2989

Please enclose a self-addressed stamped envelope for reply, or $1.00 to cover costs. If outside the USA, enclose an international postal reply coupon.

Many of Llewellyn's authors have websites with additional information and resources. For more information, please visit our website at www.llewellyn.com

from the author of **ANGEL INSIGHTS**

Angel
Intuition

A PSYCHIC'S GUIDE to
the LANGUAGE of ANGELS

TANYA CARROLL
RICHARDSON

Llewellyn Worldwide
Woodbury, Minnesota

FIRST EDITION
Fourth Printing, 2021

Book design by Bob Gaul
Cover design by Shira Atakpu
Editing by Annie Burdick

Llewellyn Publications is a registered trademark of Llewellyn Worldwide Ltd.

Library of Congress Cataloging-in-Publication Data
Names: Richardson, Tanya Carroll, author.
Title: Angel intuition : a psychic's guide to the language of angels / by
    Tanya Carroll Richardson.
Description: Woodbury : Llewellyn Worldwide, Ltd., 2018. | Includes
    bibliographical references.
Identifiers: LCCN 2018041424 (print) | LCCN 2018049896 (ebook) | ISBN
    9780738756332 (ebook) | ISBN 9780738756165 (alk. paper)
Subjects: LCSH: Angels.
Classification: LCC BL477 (ebook) | LCC BL477 .R533 2018 (print) | DDC
    202/.15—dc23
LC record available at https://lccn.loc.gov/2018041424

Llewellyn Worldwide Ltd. does not participate in, endorse, or have any authority or responsibility concerning private business transactions between our authors and the public.

All mail addressed to the author is forwarded, but the publisher cannot, unless specifically instructed by the author, give out an address or phone number.

Any internet references contained in this work are current at publication time, but the publisher cannot guarantee that a specific location will continue to be maintained. Please refer to the publisher's website for links to authors' websites and other sources.

Llewellyn Publications
A Division of Llewellyn Worldwide Ltd.
2143 Wooddale Drive
Woodbury, MN 55125-2989
www.llewellyn.com

Printed in the United States of America

Contents

Exercise List

Acknowledgments

I would like to thank the angels for being so faithful and present during the writing of this book. A very special thank you also to the angels who show up every day in intuitive sessions with my clients. I'm so grateful for family and friends, who have been extremely encouraging and supportive about my work. And thanks to Linda Konner, Angela Wix, Vanessa Wright, Annie Burdick, and Llewellyn Worldwide for making this book possible.

Disclaimer

Readers are advised to consult their doctors or other qualified health care professionals regarding the treatment of their medical or psychological concerns. Please note that the information in this book is not meant to diagnose, treat, prescribe, or substitute consultation with a licensed health care professional.

Introduction

ANGELS AND INTUITION have become an integral part of my life, so much so that I cannot imagine my existence without their constant assistance and support. Therefore, I wanted to write a book about my two favorite topics, two of the biggest, best parts of myself. My intention is that this book will help you get to know your own angels and your own intuition, because whether you realize it or not, angels and intuition are a significant part of your life too.

Not long ago, in an Angel Reading—I call my psychic sessions Angel Readings because I get most of my information from angels—a client who had bought my first angel book, *Angel Insights*, commented, "I love that in your writing, you always say you're just putting down what the angels tell you. It makes me feel like I'm reading a book written by an angel." Or more accurately, many angels!

In my sessions with clients, I spend the entire time on alert, ready to receive the messages the angels send me. Often these angelic messages, which come in very fast succession, are out of left field, or advice/insights I never would have thought of on my own. Sure, this information is being filtered through my brain and personality, so there is room for human error or miscommunication. That is why I always advise my clients to listen to my advice, but make decisions based on their own intuition and logic.

Yet in an Angel Reading with a client, or while I am sitting down to write a book like this one, I try my best to step aside and let the angels talk through me. The process is much more fun and the results are much more powerful that way. This is what I want to teach you to do in *Angel Intuition*: use your own intuition to tune into divine guidance that gives you a whole new perspective and helpful advice about whatever is happening in your life.

When I receive messages from the angels, whether in a psychic session with a client or while I am writing a book or article, I try to relay the message quickly. This helps me not to distort the message by thinking about it or second-guessing it. It's a wonderful approach to take with your own intuition. You don't always have to act on or follow intuitive guidance, but you should always sit with it and give it a chance, as opposed to immediately discounting the guidance.

After working with the exercises in this book, that approach will come more naturally to you.

So many angels helped me write this book. My guardian angels (like all of us, I have more than one) acted as coauthors, as did several archangels. Because I am working so intimately with the angels when I write, it is common for people to tell me that they feel much closer to angels while they are reading my books.

My goal is to aid you in continuing to grow that sense of intimacy with your angels even after you finish the last page. An ideal way to improve your relationship with your angels is by recognizing, using, and honing your intuition. In this book, you will grow your intuition in two ways. The first is by learning more about the mechanics of how intuition works (including taking a fun quiz to help you better understand the current state of your intuitive abilities and where your growth potential lies). Secondly, you will be given lots of exercises to help you practice using and improving your intuition. This natural human sixth sense helps you connect to angels of all kinds (guardian angels, helper angels, and archangels), as well as spirit guides, departed loved ones, and your own higher self.

Your higher self is that part of you that is connected to a Divine source of wisdom. We might also refer to your higher self as your *soul*. Your soul has some amazing answers for you. Your intuition can help you better connect to your higher self when making a big decision, like which town to move to, as well as when making smaller everyday decisions, like which grocery line will move the quickest. This book will encourage you to trust your intuition more.

One of my clients' most common questions, besides how they can get closer to their angels, is how they can improve their own intuition. The answer is no mystery, so I try to give clear guidelines here in this book—what to emphasize (chapter 7) and what to steer clear of (chapter 6) when you are working on expanding and trusting your intuition.

While this book provides helpful guidelines and general rules of angelic communication, every individual is unique, and therefore every individual's relationship with angels will be somewhat unique as well. In this book, we will cover many of the ways angels send you messages (chapter 5). No one way of angelic communication is better than another; all that matters is that an angel's message gets to you clearly—and that you recognize it as angelic advice. By leading you to examine the four "clairs," this book should help you discover how you individually receive information from your angels, and should also expand your intuitive horizons so you have more channels through which you can receive and process angelic guidance. This book will also help you discern angelic guidance from your own thoughts, fears, and desires.

Just like learning any other language, the more you practice the exercises in this book, act on angelic guidance, and develop your intuition, the more fluent you will become in the language of angels. I've become so fluent that I get paid to communicate with angels and give their messages to my clients. You might become fluent enough to change your life and live at your highest potential in your own relationships, career, calling, health, and so on. Learning the language of angels may help you be of incredible service to others and eventually become bilingual, utilizing your native tongue and the language of angels all day, every day.

When learning a new language, you want to get to know the people and culture that the language belongs to. In this case, my book will help you begin to understand angels and the dimension they inhabit, which is commonly referred to as heaven. It will also uncover how angels have the unique ability to travel easily between dimensions, often keeping one wing in heaven and one wing here on earth. Angels and humans are not really physically distant, merely separated by dimensions, a separation that exists largely in our own minds. We'll study angels in *Angel Intuition* just as you might study the people of another country or culture to better understand them.

We'll talk about who angels are, what they're like, what motivates them, their limitations, and how they can help you. I will also share with you what I have learned from the angels by speaking their language and communicating with them in my readings with clients. I will never share anything that would jeopardize my clients' anonymity, which is why many of the stories here will be from my own life or the details of the story will be altered significantly to protect the identity of any clients I mention.

I hope this book gets you more in touch with your angels, but also more in touch with your intuition, your soul, and yourself. Then you can take a quantum leap and experience your life on a whole new level. We'll expand your knowledge of the spiritual realm, reinforce important concepts you already know, ask some deep questions, and most importantly, open up your intuition so it can blossom and better help you navigate this earthly existence. Whether you are already aware of it or not, your intuition and your connection to Spirit are some of the most powerful assets you possess. And they are assets we *all* possess—each and every one of us.

LEARNING THE LANGUAGE OF ANGELS: THE FOUR CLAIRS

WHEN A CLIENT has a session with a professional intuitive, they often walk away wondering, "How did the intuitive know that?" How exactly does a professional intuitive just know things—like your age or where you're planning to go on vacation next month or the problems in your romantic relationship—with no logical explanation why? The four clairs—clairaudience (*hearing* intuitive information), clairvoyance (*seeing* intuitive information), claircognizance (*knowing* intuitive information), and clairsentience (*feeling* intuitive information)—are how psychics just know things. You are also receiving information via one or more of these pathways, whether you realize it or not. Psychics can use one, several, or all of the four clairs. Some people might be stronger or more dominant in one of the clairs than the others. I rely heavily on all four of the clairs in my readings with clients, although clairaudience (hearing intuitive information as a voice in my head) was the first of the clairs to show up regularly in my life.

Why are the four clairs the first thing we are covering in this book? If you wanted to learn how to bake a cake, the first ingredients you would be concerned with are things like flour, milk, butter, sugar, and eggs. Vanilla, chocolate, frosting, and fancy decorations would come later. In the same way, the four clairs are the foundation or building blocks of intuition.

In this chapter, I'll also share with you the story of how I came to work with angels. For most of my life, I never thought much about angels. But one day, that changed for me in a dramatic way.

Meeting an Angel Face-to-Face

I have always been very spiritual, and I have always been searching. But I never quite found my tribe, my jam, my niche … until I found angels. And the most important thing I can tell you about angels is this: Angels work with people of all faiths. In fact, angels are even there for people who have no faith, sending them guidance and working on behalf of each individual—like stagehands behind the scenes of life. Whether you are Baptist, Catholic, Unitarian, Muslim, or Wiccan, whether you worship Odin, study astrology, are drawn to Buddhism, or practice Jewish mysticism, I believe that angels are with all of you, all the time.

Before I learned about these nondenominational beings and started working with them, the concept of angels never resonated with me. I just assumed "angels" were a sweet, comforting construct from the Bible, more metaphor than fact. Spirit guides, ghosts, ascended masters, aliens, fairies—even unicorns and the Loch Ness "Monster" seemed more real. So I haven't always talked to angels. And then one day, a very ordinary day, an angel appeared before me—with wings and everything.

Angels can appear to us in many different forms: as a misty vapor, a bright white light, flashes of small colored lights, as humans, as shadows out of the corner of our eye, as clouds, in dreams or waking visions. But angels can also appear to us in the form that has long been favored by religion and popular culture: wearing flowing robes and carrying enormous, white-feathered wings on their backs.

Can you imagine looking up into the sky or up from your breakfast plate and spotting a human-looking creature rocking big feathered wings? Some of you reading this book might have had such an experience. And if so, you probably understand why angels in the Bible instruct those they appear before to "fear not." More than the oddity of a stranger with wings showing up in your home, what is most arresting about an angelic encounter of this kind is the energy that comes off of these beings. I write and speak about angels frequently, as well as rely on them heavily during my intuitive sessions with clients, but while I sit here and write about the first time I actually saw an angel, "in the flesh," so to speak, the same sacred, very intense energy I felt that afternoon over a decade ago envelops me once again. I learned later that this translucent figure who floated into my bedroom in a long, white robe and golden belt, with ringlet hair was Samantha, one of my guardian angels. But it didn't matter who this angel was to me that afternoon. All that mattered was that she was *real*. She did not say a word and floated out of the room shortly after I noticed her, but seeing is believing, and from that day on I not only believed in angels, but I also became extremely curious about them.

Since then, I have spoken with hundreds of people about their angelic encounters. And I've been blessed to discover I have a natural talent for speaking the language of angels.

The Four Clairs: How Psychics Receive Information

Every psychic pathway is unique and distinctive, so let's take a closer look at the four main ones:

Hearing Intuitive Guidance—Clairaudience

When I first saw an angel, I was already in touch with what I referred to then as "my little voice." Clairaudience is when we hear intuitive guidance as a voice in our head that is neither our own voice nor one of our own thoughts. Though this voice in my head always sounds the same, I can now tell if the voice speaking to me is an ascended master like Buddha, one of my guardian angels, or my main squeeze archangel, Archangel Michael.

Angels love to communicate with me this way, and the messages they have for clients who book Angel Readings come through loud and clear. These are messages like, "She will commit to the relationship in the fall," or that a client's divorce is especially difficult "because he's used to people leaving him." Through clairaudience I am able to intuit concrete facts about my clients, things like names, ages, and dates. I will hear a name in my mind, like "Lionel" or "Cheryl," and then have to ask my client if they know someone named Lionel or Cheryl. Sometimes it is the name of an angel coming through, but often the client will say, "That's my husband" or "That's my boss" or "That was what I named my first car!" or "That was my name in Spanish class in high school!" Another time I gave the client a name and he said, "That is the name I gave my guardian angel ten years ago!"

Timing is everything, and clairaudience helps me and my client narrow down ideal timing. In many instances, a client will say something like, "I'm thinking of signing up for a training program." Then I hear "March" in my mind, and sure enough, the client says that this program begins in March. When I hear the make and model of a car the client wants to buy, the title of the promotion they're likely to get, or what the doctor is calling that rash under their arm, it's always a bit astounding, because usually I have never even heard of that type of car, that type of job, or that type of rash! I am just repeating the words that Spirit and the angels place into my mind.

During sessions with clients, the angels love to speak clairaudiently to me using clichés: "He had a slip of the tongue."

"Old dogs can learn new tricks."

"The proof is in the pudding."

"It takes two to tango."

When I asked the angels why they prefer clichés (keep in mind that you can always ask angels questions), they told me they prefer clichés because these phrases have been so adopted by our culture that their meaning is immediate, so there is no confusing the angels' message. However, angels can also be poetic. I once asked my husband what he thought his traditional Native American name would be if he had been born into that culture, and he replied "Lone Eagle." I then wondered aloud, "What would my name be?" I immediately heard this in my mind: "Sheltering Sky."

You might experience clairaudience as you are looking at a piece of property with a realtor and hear in your mind, "This is your dream house." Maybe you have to hire someone to help you with seasonal work, and after interviewing several people, you still can't find the right fit—until you interview a candidate and keep hearing "He's the one," in your mind. Or maybe you are reading a book about subconscious financial blocks, and when you ask your angels what your biggest subconscious money block is, you hear this in your mind: "You're afraid to make more money than your mother."

Clairaudience is just one of the ways that the angels give me messages during a reading, so I am also receiving guidance via all three other clairs. Although I receive psychic messages about myself and others throughout the day, when I am in a session with a client it is like turning up the heat on a stove's burner.

"It must be overwhelming for you to walk down the street!" some people say to me, assuming that I receive messages about every stranger who passes me. While I cannot turn being psychic "off" (and I would not want to), I can turn the volume knob up and down. So don't be afraid that if you improve your intuition it will be talking to you nonstop. My clairaudient voice is extremely active during sessions with clients, because I am extremely *focused* on the client and using my intuition. My clairaudient voice is still present throughout the day, but it's not nearly as chatty!

Clairaudience: What You Need to Know

- The intuitive voice you hear in your head—clairaudience—will sound like someone actually talking. However, this voice will never be intrusive or babble on the way the human mind can!

- This voice will speak in a calm, even tone, and will always sound the same.

- Information your intuitive voice gives you could come from anyone on your spiritual guidance squad: angels, spirit guides, loved ones who have passed on, Spirit, ascended masters, or your higher self.

- Your intuitive voice will never try to scare you, but it will always give you helpful information. Occasionally this information can be a warning.

- Clairaudience and clairvoyance are some of the rarer psychic abilities, so you may not experience them on a regular basis. The more you study and hone your intuition, the more you open up the potential to experience clairaudience and clairvoyance.

- You might begin to get clairaudient messages at any point in your life, and many people report that it takes a little time to get used to.

- Voices heard by people who are mentally ill or have severe hormone or vitamin/mineral imbalances are not clairaudience.

- Clairaudient messages are usually brief and to the point.

Seeing Intuitive Guidance—Clairvoyance

Some people use the term *clairvoyant* as if it were synonymous with *psychic*, but really clairvoyance is just one of the four clairs a psychic can utilize. I feel quite like the famous fictional detective Sherlock Holmes when I am in a session with a client, and my clairvoyance is just one of my powers of deduction! Clairvoyant images are usually like a picture or movie playing in the mind's eye. Often, angels will send clairvoyant guidance that arrives as a metaphor, like a weather vane in the shape of a rooster blowing this way and that, letting me know that a client's loved one or boss is flighty and changeable. Or I might get an image of a client going through a divorce, bent over in a garden, pulling up weeds. This client is getting rid of things that no longer serve her—people, old patterns, and so on—so that she can make room for a new romance to blossom.

Sometimes I will get a clairvoyant image during a reading that is not only symbolically important to my client, but personally significant for them as well. Recently I encouraged a client to give something in his life some space and time to grow. I told him, "I'm getting an image of a sapling and it has a wooden stick behind it to support it. The angels are telling me that as this part of your life grows, your partner will be there to support you emotionally and financially—just like that stick supports the sapling." I had never gotten an image of a sapling and a stick before.

"Oh my God!" the client said. "We have these saplings growing in our front yard with sticks behind them. My wife planted them and always says, 'Won't it be amazing to see how big they grow?'"

If the client is overwhelmed, I might see them drowning or carrying some large bindle on their back. If I see an image of the continental plates shifting or the ground shaking beneath someone's feet, it means the client is experiencing such dramatic life changes that nothing feels stable. If a client is looking for a new job or business partnership, I might see them fishing, with lots of little fish swimming by their line. This might mean the client should wait for the "big fish" or the really plum offer. These are just examples. The images are usually different for every client, which makes my job fun!

Clairvoyant images might also appear outside of your mind like a projection or vision. My husband and I were out to dinner, fondly reminiscing about a family friend who had just passed. Suddenly I saw that same man appear faintly behind my husband and put his hand on my husband's shoulder (just like this man always did in life whenever he was talking to someone). This clairvoyant image let my husband and I know that our departed loved one was there and listening.

On another occasion, a friend and I were attending a benefit concert at Carnegie Hall, listening to Iggy Pop and Bernard Sumner (founding member of New Order and Joy Division) perform a phenomenal rendition of "She's Lost Control." The energy in the room was truly electric. As I listened to the song, I suddenly got a feeling that the spirit of former Joy Division front man Ian Curtis was in this famous concert hall (Ian committed suicide in 1980). Then all at once, from my vantage point high in the balcony, I saw an image of Ian's face, faint but distinctive, fill up the entire room! It was a powerful and memorable clairvoyant image that only lasted for a few seconds as I held my breath in awe.

Some clairvoyant images might be straightforward, like a picture of a hotel room sink, letting me know that's where my client lost a piece of jewelry. Clairvoyant messages can be even more straightforward, like ages and dates appearing as images in my mind. I might see the number thirty-three in my mind before I get on the phone with a client, letting me know that the client is that age right now. Occasionally I am not given the client's current age, but a formative age when something significant happened to them. I might see the number twelve in my mind and find out from the client that this was their age when they were put into foster care. These ages can be for the future too, like seeing the number forty-five and hearing from the angels that this is the age when my client will likely get remarried.

Clairvoyance: What You Need to Know

- Think of clairvoyance as communicating through pictures.

- Clairvoyant images come in a flash out of the blue, appearing fully formed in your mind.

- Clairvoyant images often use the language of metaphor. For this reason, clairvoyant images can require a bit of reflection to discern their full meaning.

- Some people will see clairvoyant visions outside of their mind. Others will even be able to see ghosts or visions of angels. If this is happening to you regularly, speak to someone you trust about how to manage this extremely rare sensitivity.

- Clairvoyance and clairaudience are some of the rarer psychic abilities. If you do not experience them, don't worry. You are still a very intuitive being! In time, you might experience them.

- Clairvoyant visions happen while you're awake, unlike dreams that occur when you're asleep. Sometimes these clairvoyant visions may come to you right before you go to sleep.

Knowing Intuitive Guidance—Claircognizance

Do you ever just know something, without any "logical" explanation for why you know it? The angels love to give me "downloads," which is when a lot of information is put into my brain instantly. These downloads come so often during a reading that it's like a rain shower of knowledge from heaven. Downloads from Spirit are especially helpful when I am trying to understand, for example, a client's complex work history or the disposition and emotional history of someone in my client's life. Claircognizance lets me understand and have instant insight into situations with lots of nuances and details.

It's wonderful when I can tell my client, "Well, you know your mother has trouble showing her emotions" or "Your boss can be so rigid," because it lets the client know I am tuning into the right person. But these are issues my client is probably already aware of. Claircognizance really helps me get underneath these issues, giving me information about peoples' real motivations. For example, maybe part of the reason my client's mother can appear emotionless and cold is because she is trying to toughen her children up to face the world, just like she was toughened up by her father, who was also highly sensitive and an alcoholic. This could make the client more open to or forgiving of her mother. Or that this rigid boss is actually being so controlling because she is afraid of all the changes currently going on in the company, and that six months from now, when things have all calmed down, will be a much better time to ask for a raise, promotion, or more flexible schedule.

Claircognizant messages can also be very simple. Maybe you're looking at possible vacation destinations with a friend— beaches, mountains, major cities—and out of nowhere you just know you should go to the Scottish Highlands. It wasn't even on your list … but somehow you're sure. Then when you arrive in Scotland, you meet your soul mate, or realize you had a past life there, or decide to base your latest book or screenplay in the Highlands, or end up investing in a piece of property, or get involved in a local charity.

A client of mine who is learning to trust and improve his intuition shared with me that he can tell the difference between his own ego thoughts and the intuitive hits that come from angels or his higher self. ("Intuitive hit" is a term psychics commonly use for a clear intuitive insight.) He said, "The intuitive thoughts come in as definitive wisdom, like, 'He was feeling betrayed by me,' instead of, 'I wonder what that guy was feeling when he said those things to me? Maybe he was feeling betrayed?' Also, the intuitive thoughts come in quickly and arrive fully formed." Now that my client is paying more attention to his intuition, these claircognizant insights are increasing.

Claircognizance: What You Need to Know

- Claircognizance often does not require any reasoning or deduction on the part of the human brain. These intuitive insights are placed into the mind fully formed.

- Claircognizance helps when we need to understand something complex very quickly.

- Claircognizance is like a download of information from Spirit onto your brain's hard drive, except this download is instantaneous.

- Aha moments or "breakthrough" realizations are examples of claircognizance.

- Sometimes claircognizant intuitive hits will be things you never could have known with your intellectual mind, like the name of a town or supplement you've never heard of before that turns out to be helpful or significant.

- With clairvoyance, you might have to take a moment to interpret the image, and with clairaudience, you might have to pause and listen. But claircognizance is understood instantly.

- This method of intuitive guidance is especially useful for inventors, therapists, scholars, artists, or anyone coming up with or requiring "breakthroughs." It's also helpful when you are trying to get beyond surface appearances to discern deeper meanings and motivations.

Feeling Intuitive Guidance—Clairsentience

My favorite way that clairsentience (when the angels give me intuitive information as a feeling) shows up in my readings with clients is when I get chills all over my body during a session. That means the client and I have hit on something very important. Another way clairsentience aids me in a reading is by helping me recognize when angels and loved ones who have passed over have entered the room. Often, when I tune into a loved one or pet who has passed over during a session with a client, I will suddenly become emotional—my voice will get choked up or tears will run down my cheeks—as I relay the departed loved one's message. This is because I am feeling that spirit's emotions very intimately and I become extremely touched by what they say.

Another way I receive clairsentient information during a reading is when I sense, through the phone line, what my client's reaction will be to a message from the angels before I say it, especially if that client's reaction will be resistance. If a new client has physical ailments, I will often feel them briefly in my own body before or during the call. If someone has bad knees, mine will ache for a few seconds, or if they have digestion issues, I will feel a sensation in my tummy. My throat will often feel tight briefly during a session if the client's throat chakra—which is where we express ourselves—is closed off. This might mean the client is not expressing their emotions to themselves or others, or that they are not asking for what they want and standing up for what they need.

I can usually get a feeling sense of the broad strokes of someone's personality before getting on the phone with them: are they reserved, bubbly, serious, compassionate, lighthearted, intellectual, creative? All this information I receive via my clairsentience.

About ten minutes before an Angel Reading begins, the energy in the room I'm in shifts and becomes more alive or palpable—that's the angels showing up for the session with my client! My clairsentience allows me to sense this energy. I also always feel so warm and lovely after a reading. It's a direct result of being, for however long the reading lasts, wrapped in a cozy blanket of angels. The angels tell me that following a reading, I am in "afterglow."

Folks have e-mailed me days after a session and written, "I'm still high off that reading!" The client is experiencing a clairsentient "buzz" from the residue of angel energy. You might also have a negative clairsentient experience if you are sensing toxic energy residue, like having trouble shaking off the energy of a fight with a family member or coworker. Energy really can "hang in the air," the angels say—for better or worse!

Clairsentience is the most common of the four clairs, and you might experience it as a gut instinct, like when you go on a first date and feel within the first fifteen minutes that this is not the partner for you, or when you walk out of the house for work and just have a feeling you've left something important behind, or when you experience a gut instinct that a project someone just put on your desk can actually wait until tomorrow.

Clairsentience also describes our intuitive ability to feel the collective energy in a room, like the collective stress in a large open-area office before a tight deadline or the collective joy of a big family wedding. Being able to tune into or sense other people's individual emotions, like looking at a smiling picture of someone on social media yet feeling an intense loneliness coming from them, is also clairsentience. If you are very clairsentient you may be easily overwhelmed by the emotions of others, almost as if you feel another person's emotions like they're your own.

The angels explain that it is natural for these highly clairsentient humans to tune into the energy of individuals, crowds, physical spaces, and even objects. Yet sometimes, the angels warn, it is "to no one's benefit" to do so. Like all super-powers, being empathic or highly sensitive/clairsentient is a super power you need to learn how to control. And like all heroes, you have to discern when to rip open your shirt and reveal the "S" beneath and when to go back into your Clark Kent mode!

The angels have this advice: When you are tuning into someone else's energy or emotions with your clairsentient intuitive muscle (which will usually happen automatically or by default), ask, "Am I gathering valuable information that might allow me to help this person? Or am I simply draining myself and going on an overwhelming energetic roller-coaster ride?"

Clairsentience: What You Need to Know

- Clairsentience is the most common of the four clairs, so it's the clair most people will experience the most often.

- Strong gut instincts or just knowing what decision to make—whether it's which dress to buy or which house to buy—fall under this category.

- Some people who are highly clairsentient might find it helpful to read books about empaths and get some tools for managing and making the most of their clairsentience.

- People who are highly clairsentient might not like crowds or being in open-area offices, because they can easily pick up on the emotions of others and the collective energy of a crowd or room. (There are tools and coping mechanisms that can help with these situations!)

- Those who are highly clairsentient might be attracted to careers as therapists, counselors, or teachers.

- Since it is the most common clair, clairsentience is probably the one that is easiest to develop or improve. So, if you start working with your intuition, expect your clairsentience to become stronger.

- Clairsentient people learn when it is helpful to tune into other people's energy and how to tune it out when it is unhelpful or overwhelming. They also learn how to protect or nourish their nervous systems.

- Clairsentient folks are also easily affected by the energy of nature—things like crystals, flowers, aromatherapy, forests, mountain ranges, or large bodies of water.

Learning a New Language Takes Time

It's vital to note that all my intuitive abilities did not present themselves at once. Clairaudience became a constant in my late twenties. A heightened clairsentience presented itself in my late twenties as well, and I remember how jarring it was at first, to suddenly feel—physically—someone else's emotions. And although I'd had clairvoyant experiences as a teenager, these intuitive images did not become a regular part of my life until my mid-thirties. I recall that when I started regularly getting these mental images loaded with meaning, I thought, "Oh, so this is what clairvoyants talk about seeing!" My claircognizance kicked in big time once I started giving professional intuitive readings a few years later. This makes sense, as it is a way for Spirit to quickly give me a ton of information so my client and I can make the most of our relatively short time together during a session.

And simply having these abilities was not enough—I had to use them and study them. Just like learning any other language, learning the language of angels takes time, patience, and practice. And just like studying a new language, you will have "breakthrough" moments with your intuition when you suddenly find yourself at a new level of understanding and communication.

After reading this book, you may begin to have clairaudient experiences in which you hear an angel in your mind, or you may simply have an increase of aha ideas, as well as an increase in synchronicities and gut instincts. No matter what your natural intuitive gifts or makeup, if you want to speak to angels and learn their language, the angels will find ways to communicate with you—every day.

Angels surround you constantly and are desperate to get your attention and send you messages. Usually angels feel like they are knocking on a door that no one ever answers. But once you learn the angel language, you will be able to open that door, let your angels in, and live at your highest potential.

ANGEL EXERCISE:

Recalling Your Encounters with the Four Clairs

One way to build your confidence regarding your intuitive or psychic ability is to identify occasions in the past when you received strong intuitive hits. The ones we remember tend to be the most dramatic examples, but once you get going with this exercise you will probably start to identify smaller, more subtle intuitive hits that you've received over the years.

Step 1. Get out a journal and something you can write with. Make sure you are in a quiet place where you can close a door to avoid distractions. Try to do this exercise when you are feeling open and relaxed.

Step 2. Record some memories of using each of the four clairs by following along in the prompts below. If you cannot remember an instance of clairaudience, for example, record an account of someone you know or someone in the news or someone in a movie experiencing clairaudience. Or wait and see if you have a memory of your own surface in a few days or weeks.

Step 3. Use this exercise to make yourself more aware of the four clairs operating in your daily life.

Clairsentience

We'll start with this clair, because it's the most common. That means you will probably find it easier to remember instances of using clairsentience.

A clairsentient memory of my own as an example:
When I went to my grandma's house in the summers as a
child, I was forever telling jokes, singing, dancing, and doing
impersonations for a large crowd of extended family members. Grandma would always comment, "Tanya, if you don't
end up on stage you have missed your calling." Whenever
she said that, which was often, it felt like a prophecy, as if
my tiny, fudge-making, domino-playing Southern grandmother was a mythical sphinx. Time seemed to slow down
when she said these words, and the energy would shift and
become heavier or more intense. I *felt* rather than thought
that this was important information. I may not be a famous
actor or musician literally on stage, but I *am* an author who
does radio interviews and personal appearances and writes
for major websites.

Record a clairsentient memory in your journal:
When you think of gut instincts, the ability to feel other
people's energy and emotions, or just the ability to feel that a
piece of information is important, what is the first memory of
yours that comes to mind? Write that down in your journal,
along with any other clairsentient intuitive hits that stick out
to you from your past.

Claircognizance

Now we'll move on to this more intellectual clair, which
involves knowing things intuitively.

A claircognizant memory of my own as an example: I had a very busy year in 2017, as I wrote two books. At the beginning of 2018, I had a lunch date planned with my agent in Manhattan and the outline and some text written for a new book, but just the thought of undertaking another big book made me feel exhausted. I still wanted a creative project for 2018, but having recently completed two books, I was a little burned out. After we gave the waitress our order, my agent turned to me and asked, "Have you ever considered doing an oracle deck?" I told her it had always been a dream of mine to create my own oracle deck.

On the subway ride back to my apartment after lunch, I kept thinking about oracle decks. Ideas were downloading into my brain rapidly, so I grabbed a pen and pad from my purse and jotted down notes as New Yorkers and tourists got on and off the subway car, which jerked in and out of stations. A name for the deck even came to me claircognizantly … and it was perfect! (It can actually take a long time to come up with the title of a book or other product, but sometimes inspiration—or really your intuition—will give you the ideal name instantly.) I began to get rapid mental downloads about the visual look of the deck, the format, the unique themes, and more. It would be fun, interesting to work on, a break from my beloved books, and so helpful to my clients. By the time I walked in the door of my apartment, I felt like—after a twenty-minute subway ride—I had the bones of the deck already.

Record a claircognizant memory in your journal:
Was there an occasion when you just knew something, without any logical explanation besides simply your own intuition? Have you ever been working on a project or pondering a problem and had large amounts of information or insight download into your brain? Take a moment and write down any claircognizant examples from your past.

Clairvoyance

Let's spend some time on the visual clair. Like the other clairs, these intuitive images will appear in your mind out of the blue, without warning or prior thought.

A clairvoyant memory of my own to get you started:
The first clear clairvoyant message I recall as an adult (that actually registered to me as a clairvoyant image) was when I was pondering some of the darkest times of my life—the day as a teen that I found out my mother had AIDS, the time when I was asked to leave her house two years later, when I found myself on my own and taking care of myself at eighteen, the loss of a significant inheritance in my twenties, someone close to me who struggled with alcoholism and suicidal thoughts (and thankfully healed from both), and struggling through illness myself in my thirties. I knew by then that angels and Spirit were always by my side, but where had they been at those very dark moments?

Suddenly I got an image in my mind of a woman floating on the ocean. She was far out at sea with no ship or help in sight, yet she was floating by clinging onto a buoy. I realized that the angels were saying, "We were the buoy. We know it wasn't fun, but we made sure you had what you needed to get through those trying times." When I looked back at each of those "low" moments in my life, I suddenly saw how there had been grace all around me that gave me what I needed to survive or keep afloat.

Record a clairvoyant memory in your journal: If you cannot recall receiving clairvoyant guidance, try asking the angels to give you guidance this way. Then pay close attention for a few weeks to any significant images appearing in your mind.

Clairaudience

Famous mystics have been reporting hearing voices for thousands of years. Spirit can talk to us in many ways, and one method is via an intuitive voice in your mind that actually sounds like someone else is speaking—but only you can hear it.

A clairaudient memory of my own to get you started: I was once reading an article about a celebrity who was dating someone decades younger than them. Part of me thought, "Good for them!" Then another part of me thought, "I don't know if I would be comfortable with such a big age gap." Suddenly a voice inside my head said, "The celebrity's kids don't like it either."

Record a clairaudient memory in your journal: Often people who do not regularly experience clairaudience will have isolated incidents of it, like hearing an angel call their name or hearing someone say "Hit the brakes!" when they need to avoid an accident.

The four clairs are some of the mechanics of mysticism, so we just got under the hood of intuition. You might also think of the clairs as human superpowers, just like your favorite fictional superhero might be able to breathe underwater or fly through the air. Understanding these four main psychic pathways will help you better recognize when your intuition is sending you messages.

2

PSYCHIC ABILITY & SENSITIVITY

WHAT DOES IT mean to be psychic? It's a common question, and one we'll explore in this chapter. While every human has a sixth sense and experiences psychic phenomena, there are also people who make their living sharing their intuition with others. Have you ever gone to see a psychic or a healer who relied heavily on their intuition? In this chapter I want to share some of my own experiences with psychics, from my first psychic reading at sixteen to the psychic in Paris who cleared my throat chakra and then took me out for crepes and a magical walk around the City of Light at midnight. Because my clients trust me with their most personal issues, I will rely mainly on stories from my own life or significantly change the personal details of stories involving my clients. If you haven't worked closely with psychics before, this chapter will give you an idea of what to look for in a psychic.

Whenever I tell a stranger that I'm a professional psychic, they often look at me with awe. "That's so interesting!" they usually say. I get the sense that people suddenly see me as much more mysterious—and maybe not even a normal human! In sharing with you what my abilities are and some of my personal history about when my abilities presented themselves, I'm hoping you will see that psychic ability—while fascinating—is actually more normal than we realize. Maybe you'll even recognize yourself in one of my stories and discover that you have more psychic ability than you thought. I can assure you that we *all* have tons of psychic potential, something we will discuss later in this book.

Since most people who are attracted to psychics are what I call "sensitive," I want to explore this topic by describing sensitive people, or my typical clients. I find that many sensitive people have known they were different since childhood, but some do not understand their sensitivity, realize how to manage it, or know how to utilize it fully to their advantage. The chapter also ends with a fun sensitivity quiz ... but don't skip ahead! (I love quizzes, so I understand the temptation.)

I've Always Been Attracted to Psychics

The notion of a mystic who could peel back the veil, tell me deeper truths about life and my soul, and maybe even see into my past, present, and future always resonated with me. It never sounded fake or outlandish. From the first time I heard about psychics while watching a TV documentary on the topic when I was around eleven years old, no part of me questioned or was skeptical. I wanted to know more! Now I always tell clients: If you are drawn to something, if it really resonates with you or interests you, explore it. This can be your soul giving you clues to a life purpose or calling—or simply an aspect of your soul that wants to reveal and express itself.

Back in sixth grade, I got so excited about the documentary on psychics that I tried to do experiments to test my psychic ability, just like the psychic institute did on TV. With the help of my brother, I discovered that I could correctly guess the color of flash cards with uncanny accuracy. While I would close my eyes, my brother would turn his back and pick a yellow, green, red, or blue card. I knew the color of the card he was holding because the color would appear in my mind. If my brother tried to trick me and pull two cards at once, I would see two colors in my mind.

However, the first time I made an appointment to talk with a psychic, I was nervous. Terrified, actually. I was sixteen and in my junior year of high school. An adult friend of the family used this psychic regularly and gave me her business card. I believe now that this unique opportunity fell into my lap at a young age because Spirit placed it there.

Yet when I arrived at the psychic's home for my first appointment, I stood on her porch, staring at the deceptively ordinary front door, trying to work up the nerve to knock. My heart thudded as if it were pumping raw emotion. Finally, I knocked and heard someone stir inside. I think I half expected this woman to shoot lasers out of her eyes, or at least be able to read my every thought. Instead she opened the door with a kind, bright smile. She was dressed normally

and casually in sweats—no gypsy headscarf or big hoop ear-
rings (although aren't those great?). As she walked me into
her living room, she didn't carry herself like Gandalf or the
Lady of Avalon—her energy was sweet and gentle. She sat
me down at a table covered in a pretty cloth with two chairs.
"Would you mind waiting just a minute, dear?" she asked. "I
have some laundry I need to put into the dryer." Well that
brought it all down to earth!

This experience has given me enormous compassion for
anxious clients who come to their first reading with me. Like
with my first reading all those years ago, the nerves wear off
in the initial five to fifteen minutes or so of a reading. Many
people fear psychics are going to tell them something terrible. But a good psychic should be able to make you feel
relaxed and safe.

One thing a psychic reading does is let you know what
your highest potential is in a situation or relationship. Yes, psychics are there to warn you of pitfalls you might avoid ahead,
but the majority of every reading should be both healing and
inspirational. Sometimes there are inconvenient truths the
client may not be excited to hear, but these are always delivered by me with love, mercy, and a lack of judgment.

I continued seeing this psychic I was referred to at sixteen all through high school and into my early twenties. She
was the first person to suggest I become a writer. Once during a session, she stopped talking mid-sentence and her eyes
opened wide as if she'd just had an aha idea. She turned to the

bookcase behind her, grabbed a title on creative writing, and handed it to me solemnly.

"You need to read books on creative writing and get in the habit of writing regularly," she told me. I was already in college and had no intention or notion of being a writer when she made these suggestions. It's a wonderful example of how a professional psychic or intuitive can encourage you to grow in a new, healthy direction and bring forth sides of yourself that are currently dormant.

This psychic also warned me of serious issues someone close to me would have, years before they manifested, which made it easier to deal with the problem when it became full-blown. And whenever I was facing a big change or major decision that I felt scared or unsure about—whether it was breaking up with a boyfriend or picking a minor in college—I would book a session and talk the matter through with my psychic. Not only would she give me practical advice, but she also gave me a lot of confidence.

Of course, not everything this psychic predicted came true. I remember she once told me I would teach English as a second language while living in another country. But then again, psychics predict possibilities, not certainties. It definitely could have happened. After she predicted this, I ended up minoring in German. I also did live abroad in England for a few years (which she predicted long before I considered it).

While enrolled in graduate school in London, I saw a wonderful psychic at a psychic institute after attending a lecture there. "Do you like the Brontës?" she asked at one point in a lilting Welsh accent.

"Very much!" I said. "*Wuthering Heights* and *Jane Eyre* are two of my favorite books."

The psychic nodded knowingly. "Well, I think you are connected to the Brontës from a past life."

As an aspiring writer at that point, I was more than intrigued. "Are you saying I was one of the Brontë sisters in a past life?" I asked hopefully.

"No," the psychic replied. "But I think you were one of their servants."

This comment was more believable and pretty funny! Still, my face fell.

"A treasured, very loved servant," she amended. "You were close to the family." Many years later on our honeymoon, my husband and I stopped off at Haworth, the village in northern England where the Brontë sisters lived. When we set out to walk on the moors, it was cold, windy, and raining. But we were only there for the day, so we trudged on.

"My throat is still sore from that cold I picked up," my husband said at last. "I hate to say this but we should turn back." As soon as we reluctantly began walking back to the village, the wind and rain stopped on a dime. We stared at each other, both having a woo-woo feeling that something supernatural was involved. We ended up wandering the moors for hours.

I remember walking out of the psychic session in London feeling so much lighter. Being around people who talked about spirits and past lives felt like being home. This psychic was the first person who ever identified anyone on my spiritual guidance squad, the team of angels, spirit guides, and dead loved ones who watch over each one of us. "You have a Native American spirit guide named Feather Cloud," she told me. Having someone specific in the spirit world to think about, pray to, or connect with was a big shift for me.

When I moved to New York City, I saw psychics here and there, even paying top dollar for a session with a "celebrity" psychic. Then, in my mid-thirties I wanted to start seeing someone regularly again for general advice. The deeper call, which I did not realize at the time, was that my intuitive abilities were becoming more developed and I needed a guide or mentor. When clients say they suddenly feel very strongly about investing in something, whether it's a hobby, a wellness practice, an exercise regime, career training, or their relationships with loved ones, it is often a soul nudge.

The psychic I began seeing in my mid-thirties was recommended by a friend, and has become a trusted confidant, someone I speak with two or three times a year. (Some people are shocked to hear that a person who gives intuitive readings professionally sees another intuitive. It's kind of like how every therapist sees a therapist.) My current psychic was also the first psychic to ever hint that I would begin giving readings myself.

"Your intuition is getting so strong that you will receive information about people just by meeting them or seeing a picture of them," she told me during a session. "It will be a little overwhelming at first, but don't worry. You will get used to it."

A year later, after I had begun offering Angel Readings, my psychic said, "Have you ... did you start ... are you giving people readings now?" I wanted to see if she would intuit it ... and she did!

Why had no one predicted this for me before? My mother once saw a psychic when I was in middle school who told her I would be famous (still waiting for that one). But I imagine that no other psychic told me I would become a psychic because it was not yet time for me to hear the information. If we are given information before we are ready it can negatively affect our choices. What if the psychic I saw when I was sixteen told me I would be a psychic one day? I might never have gone to graduate school for writing or trained as a writer at magazines and newspapers. I would have missed out on a key part of my destiny, one that obviously had to come first and is tied to my calling as an intuitive (considering as of now I have published five nonfiction books about spirituality, and writing gives me great joy).

No two psychics are the same. Usually they are strong in one, a few, or all of the four clairs. Some also employ tarot or oracle cards. Others use numerology. Psychics might incorporate astrology. Perhaps they see auras or work with energy.

There are also people who channel one spirit, or a group of spirits, who talk through the psychic or medium. Others specialize in speaking with people who have died and passed over. I work primarily with angels. I have been to all types of psychics (certainly all the types I mentioned here), and they were each fascinating, informative, and distinctive.

One thing I would mention as a cautionary tale are the people who have a sign out on the street, something like "Palm Readings for $10." There is nothing wrong with advertising or seeing people off the street (at least in theory). When I first moved to New York City I was told of a cafe in Manhattan where psychics hung out and you could walk in off the street and get a short twenty-minute reading for thirty dollars over a cup of herbal tea. I received a wonderful and very accurate reading at this psychic cafe from a young woman with beautiful olive skin, sparkling eyes, and a sensuously deep voice who sat in a booth across from me. Some of what she told me that rainy afternoon didn't make much sense at the time, but she was predicting things and warning me of things that came true years later (I still marvel today at the accuracy of this reading).

You can get a terrific reading from someone you meet "cold" or from a sign on the street. But it might be ideal to meet a psychic through a referral (via a friend or relative who had a session with them), or after reading some testimonials from the psychic's clients or articles the psychic has written.

Can You Tell If a Psychic Is "Real"?

"How many of these psychics are scam artists?" a friend asked me recently.

The unsaid implication in his question was, "I believe you are for real, but most of these other people have to be faking it, right?"

The angels quickly answered him clairaudiently in my own mind, saying that scam artists in this industry really are "few and far between." I think the vast majority of people working in this field are kind-hearted, well-meaning folks with genuine intuitive ability. Their abilities, experience, and skill sets may vary widely, however.

Skeptics want to believe—and try to prove—that all psychics are scam artists. Besides being wrong, this theory is also incredibly closed-minded. The angels are reminding me that there was a time when people called it a crazy theory that some illnesses are caused by tiny germs you cannot see with the naked human eye.

There is a chemistry between us and anyone we bring into our lives: friends, mates, health-care professionals, coworkers, clients, and intuitives. That is why you might have a friend rave about her reading with a psychic, but just feel "meh" after your reading with the same psychic. Psychics can also convey inconvenient truths that people are not ready or willing to hear (inconvenient truths are not just relegated to documentaries about climate change). This can lead someone to claim that the psychic was "way off base." And even the best psychics *can* sometimes just be plain old wrong about an issue.

You might be going to a psychic seeking information you should be getting from another type of professional. For example, there are some medical intuitives who work with doctors to help diagnose patients. But the psychic I went to see many years ago was not one. She was a reputable, experienced professional with a good client base, and she gave me some amazing insight into the future of my career as a writer. She also shared with me some seemingly minor insights, which turned out to be uncannily correct years later.

Yet I sought out that psychic not for advice about my career or general happiness, but for insight about my health—which was quickly unraveling. I had resisted seeing doctors or healthcare professionals up until that point, hoping I could handle the crisis myself (I now realize how ridiculous and naïve that was). Despite this overall accurate reading, everything she said about my health was misleading. And I knew it even as I was hearing her say it. This reading pushed me to finally seek out healthcare providers who specialized in my symptoms/condition. When I ask the angels now about this reading, they tell me the psychic was "definitely" giving me the wrong information just so I could realize that a psychic was not the person to go to for this sort of help. "Trickster energy" was at work, and it helped point me to the correct path. We'll explore more of the trickster's role in intuition later in this book.

For every thing a good psychic is off about or the client chooses to handle differently than the psychic's advice, there should be several things the psychic is "right" or "on" about. No one can completely predict the future. The future is a combination of an individual's free will, the free will of others, events that were fated, and a larger world with forces that are constantly changing and in flux. In other words, a lot can happen!

The angels are showing me a clairvoyant image of a leader surrounded by advisors. Having a trusted psychic is like a world leader adding another member to their cabinet or counsel. The psychic's is just one expert opinion the leader should take under advisement.

What to Look For in a Psychic:

1. **Non-judgmental:** Psychics should be supportive and compassionate, never condemning. This allows the client to open up and feel safe being vulnerable.

2. **Open-minded:** During a session, I show respect for a client's spiritual belief system. If they are a devout Christian or a devout Pagan, for example, I will make sure the session honors their belief system.

3. **Inspiring:** Psychics should encourage you to make positive changes in your life. A psychic strongly advised me a few years ago to start writing fiction again. I had dropped this hobby for over a decade and realized how much I missed it after her recommendation.

4. **Empowering:** A great psychic will remind you that your own intuition is powerful and will push you to

make your own decisions after weighing all of the input during a session, including the psychic's suggestions.

5. **Out of the box:** Look for a psychic who tells you things you never would have thought of on your own, alerting you to new attitudes, options, and opportunities.

6. **Revealing:** We all have subconscious issues and patterns that are self-sabotaging. Your psychic should alert you to some of yours and help you get to the root cause of these issues so you can begin to heal and shift the patterns.

7. **Makes sense of the past and present:** Everyone wants to know about their future! But remember, some things in the future are unwritten. The past very much informs your present and future; part of a psychic's job is to help you make sense of the events and motivations from your past and present.

8. **Never pushy:** If a psychic is trying to push you into booking your next session or saying you have to come back at a certain time, proceed with caution. They might just be trying to genuinely help you or build up their practice (we all have to earn a living). But when and how often you see a psychic is entirely up to you.

9. **Displays accuracy:** Recently a client told me, "Remember that thing you said would happen in our last session? Well, it happened exactly as you described!" No one bats a thousand and this is an imperfect science, but your psychic should display enough accuracy to keep you coming back.

10. **Goes deep:** One definition of a lightworker is someone who goes into dark places to bring more light. Psychics should never shy away from a client's difficult or painful issues and experiences.

11. **Ensures confidentiality:** Many psychics get new clients through word-of-mouth, so they could end up being the go-to psychic for several members of the same family. Whatever is said during a session should stay only between the psychic and the client. If you have concerns, don't be afraid to bring them up and get clarification.

12. **Comfortable:** Many people find their psychic through a friend's recommendation or by reading a blog post or article the psychic has written. Follow your instincts when choosing a psychic, but you can also do a little research on a prospective psychic first. Getting a psychic through a recommendation or researching them ahead of time will help you feel more open and comfortable during a session.

13. **Humble**: Psychics are human and therefore not always right! Humility is a very important quality to look for in any healer you work with. And remember, someone can be very confident in their abilities and still be humble.

14. **Practical**: I like to give my clients a sense of who is on their spiritual guidance squad and how to connect with them. But I also pride myself on providing clients with very practical advice about the next steps for improving their lives.

Harnessing the Power of Your Intuition

There are many things that can cause our intuition to blossom, which is certainly what happened to me as an adult. These include:

Recognizing the world as a magical place: Realize that the universe talks back to us in the form of signs and synchronicities. This is real, and not merely wishful thinking or something you are making up. The universe is more complex, alive, and interactive than we imagine.

Developing gratitude for the simplest things: This increases awareness of the present moment, which helps you to stay mindful and recognize intuitive guidance from your angels. Stop and notice what you have to be grateful for in your life every day.

Engaging in a two-way conversation with the universe: Ask the universe a question, keep your senses alert, and you will receive clear, powerful guidance. Sometimes this guidance will come immediately. Other times you may have to wait days or even weeks. If this is the case, be patient. The right message will come at the right moment. This is called divine timing.

Following the universe's lead: Sometimes the universe knows best and will change the conversation on you! Always follow its lead. This is what I have learned to do both in psychic readings with clients and in my personal life. The universe will always present you with guidance about what is most pressing in your life right now. You might be looking for signs about how to improve your health or attract a romantic partner, and instead receive signs about how you need to switch jobs or move homes.

Learning how authentic guidance feels: When you get a strong sign from Spirit and the angels—whether it's via one of the four clairs or one of the other common ways that Spirit and the angels send you signs (which we will cover later in the book)—the guidance resonates somewhere deeper even than your gut. It resonates in your soul. Time seems to slow, as if the moment lingers and the energy around you feels more alive. You might get chills or have the hair on your arms stand on end or experience a sinking or giddy feeling in your stomach. Signs from the universe will also stay with you, so you will often catch yourself still thinking about the sign days later.

Living and eating clean: In my book *Angel Insights*, I talk about the Third Eye Diet, which basically means eating more mindfully. Limiting caffeine, sugar, and alcohol. Eating organic food and clean, cruelty-free animal products. Switching to this diet fifteen years ago increased my intuition exponentially. I began to have clear, regular clairaudient messages from Spirit and the angels, and a heightened clairsentience. Additionally, getting the right supplements, vitamins, and minerals that your nervous system needs to perform at top levels will aid your intuition, as it is closely linked to your nervous system. That's why proper rest and avoiding unnecessary stress will also boost your intuition.

Whether you are highly intuitive and have many psychic experiences on a regular basis, or are reading this book thinking, "Nothing like that has ever happened to me," your intuition will improve significantly if you play with it and practice. Just like carpenters get better at the craft the more they practice their trade, the more clients I've seen over the years, the more accurate I've become. But you don't have to be a professional psychic to have a rockin' intuition that helps you live at your full potential in all areas of your life—like health, finances, career, relationships, romantic love, and being of service in the world.

I have a client who has been practicing using his intuition more—and is getting great results. If he has a dilemma at home or work, he now asks himself, "What does my intuition have to say?" Get in the habit of asking your intuition for advice, along with all the other cabinet members on your council (your emotions, your intellect, your past experiences in the world), when faced with a question.

Are You Highly Sensitive?

While my clients come from all walks of life, one common thread is that they are usually highly sensitive. It's very easy for these folks to absorb the energy or emotions of other people, because they can naturally tune into another person's energy so easily and so adeptly that they feel it as though it's their own. This is commonly referred to as being *empathic*.

I read a client once who was so empathic that when a loved one who lived on the other side of the country got the flu, she got the flu too! She admitted that because she was so sensitive to other people's feelings and emotions, the world could be pretty overwhelming. "I hide out a lot," she said. "You must be this way too? How do you handle it?"

I *am* empathic as well. It's easy for me to tell when someone is hurting and I have a natural desire to try to talk it through with them or make them feel better. When you can feel other people's emotions you want to help others more, which is why so many empathic people go into the healing arts (although being empathic can also give you a predisposition to codependency or trying to manage other people's emotions).

Long before I started giving psychic readings, people would seek me out as someone they could tell their troubles to or receive a pep talk from. When I worked in a large office, folks were always coming over to me to unload. "I don't know what it is," I told my boss, "but people want to confide in me." If you are highly sensitive or empathic you have probably had the same experience with family, friends, coworkers, and even strangers. I was also nicknamed "the diplomat" by family members and coworkers, because I could always see where another person was coming from and express, explain, or interpret their motives.

I believe empaths or people who are sensitive to energy need to know this about themselves, and simply adjust their lifestyle a bit. Sensitive folks definitely need to work on energetic and emotional boundaries. Archangel Raphael, the healing archangel, tells me that anytime you need help with boundaries, you can call on him or Archangel Michael, the boundary king! The angels are reminding me of the ancient Greek maxim, "know thyself." These words were carved into the stone of the Temple of Apollo at Delphi. Simply knowing and accepting that you are highly sensitive will help you manage this sensitivity.

Being highly sensitive really means being hyperperceptive. Because sensitive people pick up on the slightest shift in the energy or emotions of others, sensitive people are more easily overwhelmed, simply because they are perceiving more.

Coping Skills for Sensitivity

The following are some real-world ways to navigate life if you suspect you are highly sensitive:

Learn about your sensitivity. Books like this one, or those with the words *sensitive* or *empathic* in the title should help you to better understand your disposition and make you realize you are far from alone!

Accept that you have different limits for stimulation. You might have a friend that can work in a busy hospital all day and then go out at night with a group of coworkers and finally come home to call her sister for a heart-to-heart. Highly sensitive people can be introverts or extroverts, but they cannot handle as much stimulation as people who are not as sensitive.

Build in recovery time. If a highly sensitive person was on a retreat with a bunch of other seekers, or at a large family reunion, they would probably want to build in some quiet time alone each day so their nervous system could settle back down. I once knew someone who toured in a band, and as soon as the group got to a new town this musician would jump out of the van and go for a walk around alone. This musician claimed to be "seeing the sights," but was actually a sensitive person taking a break from being in a van with a bunch of other people all day. Get in the habit of building in this downtime each day no matter what is going on. It will help you get your nervous system idling on neutral again.

Teach the people in your life to respect your sensitivity, but don't expect a free pass on anything. If your partner or roommate is not so sensitive, they need to know how and why you are different. That goes for close friends and family members too. And no teasing allowed about being sensitive! Sensitive people can get their feelings hurt easily, even if they are tough and do not like to show when they are hurt. In turn, get to know the people in your life and their special needs—we all have them. And remember, being sensitive does not mean you need to hide away or be treated as something precious. Likewise, being sensitive does not give you the excuse to opt out of difficult situations or conversations. It does *not* make you better, more interesting, more enlightened, more spiritual, or more worthy than anyone else.

Find ways to have better emotional and energetic boundaries. I was once on the phone with a celebrity psychic who said, "You're like a sponge! As soon as you walk into a room you just absorb it all." How many of you can relate? It's not a curse or a talent. Just a wiring issue that has its benefits and drawbacks. Learn how *not* to tune into people, as tuning in is probably second nature for you. Consider looking into shielding or energy clearing for tips, and read up about codependency so you know what to avoid. Now that I give readings professionally myself, I'm so much better about not absorbing everything. People often comment on how calm and grounded I seem, and it's honestly how I usually feel inside (although trust me, I have my challenging days).

Practice rockstar-level self-care. The best way to protect your sensitivity is to make sure you're getting what you need: rest, play, great food and supplements, the chance to be of service, activities to engage your mind and soul, and lots of love. That is your strongest shield. Respecting and honoring your sensitivity is central to your self-care.

Embrace routine. Too much routine can be boring and stifling, but by and large the human nervous system loves routine. Highly sensitive people are especially drawn to building a steady rhythm for their days, which is calming to their sensitive nervous systems. This is why some of my clients seem to have taken holy orders in past lives, like being nuns or monks. Besides being attracted to spiritual pursuits, a quiet life of discipline and order can be very appealing to the highly sensitive!

Spend time in nature. Highly sensitive people are perceptive enough to pick up on the grounding energy of nature. They are moved by its beauty and calmed by sensing Spirit's eternal handprint on nature. Spending time with animals might also be something highly sensitive people are particularly drawn to doing.

Avoid caffeine. I often get on the phone with a new client who is extremely sensitive and have the angels tell me they need to quit caffeine. "I'm hearing that you drink four cups of coffee a day," I might say. Other times they are only drinking one cup, which can still be too much for some people. Or the client might love black tea. Keep in mind that even green tea has caffeine. Some clients can handle one cup of coffee in the morning. Others should probably switch over to decaf coffee and decaf tea exclusively. Sensitive people typically only need a little of something to feel it, and a bunch of caffeine is like a jolt of power that can overload those sensitive circuits.

Recognize when you are overstimulated. Because sensitive people pick up on more, they are more quickly overstimulated. Get to know yourself so you can recognize when you are frazzled or overwrought. Then take immediate steps to get yourself back to neutral (be patient with yourself, as it takes the sensitive nervous system longer to settle back down). Play a game with yourself by working backward to see what events, people, interactions, or self-care missteps led to this feeling of being frazzled.

Folks who are sensitive to energy can have difficulty speaking up for themselves and expressing their needs. This comes up regularly with clients in my Angel Readings. If an energy-sensitive client senses that their request or opinion has caused anxiety, disappointment, anger, confusion, sadness, or even resistance in another person, the client will back down rather than expose themselves to feeling—secondhand—this uncomfortable emotion. Many times, the sensitive person will pick up on how the other individual is going to react or will have a fear about how they will react, and therefore have enormous *anticipatory* stress about confronting people.

I think sensitive people are more prone to anticipatory stress about any situation, so the build-up to an event like a wedding is way more stressful than the event itself. Sensitive people can also be more prone to perfectionism, as their sensitivity makes them loathe to "cause a mistake." This often makes sensitive people exceptional employees.

Are sensitive people more compassionate? I think it's not that simple. When you can actually feel someone else's emotion, it makes you less inclined to hurt people, but that does not mean you are a better or more bighearted person. You are just more sensitive, and in some ways this desire not to hurt others is self-preservation! Some people who are labeled as "pushovers" are really just energy-sensitive.

Are people who are highly sensitive more naturally intuitive? There *is* a link, because sensitive people pick up on energy quicker and easier than other folks. They can sense the subtleties in life. So it would therefore follow that sensitive people would pick up on even subtle intuitive hits more readily.

Sensitive people can be reserved, or be very open, or be very emotionally intense. Some sensitive people might cope with their sensitivity by becoming withdrawn or emotionally remote (sometimes clients in a session will describe one of their parents as "cold," though the angels inform me that this relative is actually quite sensitive). Other sensitive types might cope by being brash or even cruel, pretending to be completely oblivious to the feelings of others as a way to try and desensitize or "numb" themselves (other numbing techniques for sensitive people are alcohol and drugs or any sort of addiction that takes them out of the present moment, even shopping). Use your intuition, not just someone else's words or actions, to decide if a person in your life is highly sensitive. Who was the first person (or people) who came to mind when you read that sentence?

Being sensitive is not code for being "weak," although I think many sensitive people do have a more *delicate* nervous system. We should think of sensitivity as a "superpower," one that should not only be used, but also needs to be understood and protected. The angels are giving me images of a young Superman from the movies and comic books. Often when superheroes are young or just discovering their powers, they get into trouble, have lots of accidents, and find their super-power frustrating. But you can master sensitivity in time, become friends with it, and use it to your advantage just as Clark Kent did. The angels are reminding me with visual images from the 1980 movie *Superman* II that the only time Clark Kent gets into real trouble is when he tries to give up or deny his powers. He has them for a reason, and so do you. If sensitivity is not one of your superpowers, rest assured that you have others. We all do!

Now that I conduct professional psychic readings, my sensitivity has increased and I will often tear up instantly when confronted with a touching news article or a poignant line of dialogue in a movie. If you or your child is the same, don't ever label this behavior—even to yourself—as ridiculous or embarrassing, or shame it in any way. This can cause the throat chakra to become restricted and lead to difficulty expressing emotions. If your emotions ever become overwhelming, seek out a trained counselor or other healthcare professional to help.

Sensitive Children

Sensitive children may have different limits or need different routines than other kids at school or at home. Beyond having psychic phenomenon occur around junior high school, I myself became very sensitive in general during this period, and I started to wonder if inanimate objects had feelings. I also became extremely concerned about the suffering I saw not only among my peers, but also on TV or in the news. You might look back on your own life and pinpoint times when your sensitivity became heightened. Back then I didn't know what this sensitivity was or that it presented itself more heightened in me than what was considered normal—so I just went with it.

Many clients who come to me have a sensitive child in the house. It is common for a client with two children, for example, to have those children appear to me as salt and pepper shakers clairvoyantly. One child might be highly sensitive, while their sibling from the same gene pool is not so sensitive (although note that, again, sensitive people can be either introverted, extroverted, or somewhere in the middle).

If sensitive children are in a very dysfunctional home, they can try to hide or shut down their sensitivity.

My advice for parents of a sensitive child is to research sensitivity and know that your sensitive child is a little different and may require special rules and handling. They might want to talk more about their emotions or be easily overwhelmed by their emotions; they could have very active imaginations and scare easily; they may care a great deal what others think or get their feelings hurt more readily; they might have fewer but closer friendships; they may be more clingy; they might crave more alone or retreat time; and they might talk about Spirit and angels.

Keep in mind, though, that every sensitive child will be unique, because sensitivity, like intuition, can exist on a spectrum or present itself differently in each individual. But then again, aren't all children wonderfully unique?

Quiz:
Recognizing Sensitivity in Yourself and Others

Simply recognizing that you or someone close to you is sensitive is half of the equation, so I devised this fun sensitivity quiz. Hopefully your answers to these questions will help you gauge your sensitivity or that of your child or spouse (you can take the quiz and answer as you imagine someone you love would). Answer each question with either: always, often, or sometimes/rarely.

1. Are you sensitive to the pain and feelings of others, almost to the point that you can experience their pain or joy as if it were your own?

2. Do you get a sense of when to tune out the energy of others because you are aware of when you are reaching a level of overwhelm?

3. Do you have coping skills for when you feel overwhelmed by the energy and emotions of others, like going for a walk, going to another room, or reading a book to put yourself in a different headspace?

4. Did you always take the side of the underdog when you were little?

5. Does the mistreatment of people and animals bother you greatly?

6. Do you regularly take realistic action steps, like donating time or money to people in need?

7. When you see someone suffering on TV or in the news, do you often go back and think of them later in the day?

8. Are you an activist of any kind?

9. When you see someone homeless on the street, is your first impulse to help, without ever subjecting them to judgment or questions?

10. When you have been at a celebration like a party or a wedding, do you find that you need some alone time afterward to calm down and find your center, even if you had a blast?

11. After a big weekend of social engagements, do you then need one or two weekends "off"?

12. Do you have general guidelines about how many social engagements you make in a week or month?

13. Do you often prefer to meet with friends one on one or in very small groups?

14. Are you sensitive to caffeine and alcohol, almost as if these substances affect you more than they seem to affect others?

15. Is having quiet time very important to you?

16. Do you struggle with how much time to spend with people versus how much time to spend alone?

17. Do you sometimes miscalculate and spend so much time alone that you feel isolated?

18. Do people seem to seek you out to tell their troubles to or are you known in your circle as a good listener?

19. Do you like to take your time with work projects and don't like to be rushed?

20. Are you a perfectionist or detail-oriented?

21. Do you emotionally bond with people very quickly?

22. Are you known as someone who can "read" people?

23. Do you often arrive very early to potentially stressful situations like airport terminals, work conferences, sold-out movies, etc.?

24. Have you been accused of crying too easily?

25. Do fictional characters feel almost alive to you, so that you can be extremely moved or affected by movies, books, plays, and operas?

26. Are you deeply moved by beauty?

27. Is it important that your environment at home and work is clean, neat, and calm?

28. Are soft music or nature sounds especially soothing to you?

29. Is sitting or walking in nature a surefire way to calm you down or cheer you up?

30. Are you easily overstimulated, so that a piece of information or an event will have you feeling excited or restless long after others have "moved on"?

31. Do you ever have racing thoughts?

32. Do you often give people the benefit of the doubt or have trouble judging others?

33. Is emotional exhaustion more common for you than physical or even mental exhaustion?

34. Are you known as a "worry wart"?

35. Are you sensitive to chemicals and junk food?

36. Are you more nervous than most about taking physical risks like getting surgery or riding a roller coaster?

37. Do you avoid scary movies?

38. Can you feel heartbroken easily?

39. Do your feelings get hurt easily?

40. Do you often get a "feeling" about things? For example, you know that someone is upset or happy before you even call and hear their news?

41. Do you anticipate the feelings of others, sometimes making it difficult for you to muster up the courage to confront people or have difficult conversations?

42. Do you sometimes avoid conflict even when you know it would be healthy and productive?

43. Is it easy for you to see all sides of a situation or be able to "get" where other people are coming from?

44. Do you often anticipate what could go wrong in a situation and take action steps to prevent mishaps, while others think you are being too cautious?

Interpreting your quiz results (be sure to read all the categories, no matter your answers)

Grape skin sensitivity (your answers were mostly "always"): When I speak with a first-time client who is extremely sensitive, the angels often give me this information by showing me an image of a grape. The skin of a grape is very thin, and one way to describe sensitive people is thin-skinned (although that unfortunately has negative connotations that you and I do not subscribe to). Thin-skinned really means that these folks absorb a lot.

When I tell most extremely sensitive clients that the angels have indicated that they are very sensitive, the client will laugh and reply, "Oh, yes, that's true!" So generally these folks are aware of their sensitivity and probably have been since childhood.

Sometimes this level of sensitivity can be overwhelming, especially if you have not studied sensitivity and learned how to protect yourself. I think simply the energy of other people—an anxious boss, for example—can be overwhelming if the extremely sensitive person is near the anxious boss, even if they are not directly interacting.

Read up on this subject of sensitivity, as there are many coping skills at your disposal! Sensitive people are often thoughtful and reflective, so they will enjoy learning more about themselves! Angels and Spirit can be very real to these folks, to the point that they might see or hear angels and people who have passed over. Extremely sensitive people do not have to isolate, and can experience full, happy lives!

In my experience, these extremely sensitive people can be intensely compassionate souls. Just make sure that if you fall in this category of sensitivity that you do not let others dominate you because it feels easier than standing your ground and dealing with disappointing or upsetting the people around you.

Examples of people in the grape-skin sensitivity category in pop culture might include the character Jon Snow from *Game of Thrones*, the late Princess Diana, commentator Van Jones, musician Stevie Nicks, and author Lorna Byrne.

Apple skin sensitivity (your answers were mostly "often"): The apple has a slightly thicker skin than the grape, and with this level of sensitivity people are mainly aware that they can pick up subtlety easier than most, but have a stronger natural barrier between themselves and the rest of the world than those in the grape-skinned sensitivity category.

Folks in this medium-sensitive category might be speaking to someone and get the sense that this person is thinking the opposite of what they are saying. They may glance at a coworker and get the feeling that this calm-looking coworker is really very upset inside.

I once asked a sensitive client if she was open to the idea of past lives or if past lives resonated with her, and the client said, "I'm open to anything." Many sensitive people are open-minded and spiritually curious. This is probably because they are able to pick up on things not quite of this world or are more in touch with their sixth sense. The angels tell me that many people who are seekers and read books like mine fall into this apple-skin sensitivity category. They might be drawn to careers where they interact closely with other people, like counseling, nursing, teaching, social work, acting, or TV interviewing. People in the apple-skin category might fear that this level of intimacy at work would be overwhelming, but that is absolutely not true—once they have the right coping skills.

Examples of people in the apple-skin sensitivity category in pop culture might include the character Gillian Owens in *Practical Magic*, TV personality Kathie Lee Gifford, athlete LeBron James, comedian Ellen DeGeneres, and late singer/actress Judy Garland.

Banana peel sensitivity (you answered mostly "sometimes/rarely"): Folks in this category can be just like a banana—you might have to peel back the layers to find the sensitivity inside. People who are uncomfortable with their sensitivity, are hiding their sensitivity, or simply have a strong "warrior" archetype in their soul can fall into this category. Sometimes folks who appear to be "tough cookies"—very strong, capable, and grounded, or in some cases, even cold—can possess this banana-peel sensitivity. Just like the banana, the hardiness on the outside does not quite match what is on the inside—something much mushier.

If you are reading this book, it means you are attracted to things like angels, intuition, and sensitivity, which makes you more sensitive than many. Your challenge may be opening up to your sensitivity and feeling safe to do so, which many in the banana peel category do very successfully. Being sensitive does not have to make you feel vulnerable. It can actually be empowering! Your tougher exterior might suit you, your circumstances or challenges, and your life purpose. People in this category can accomplish great things in life and might have large soul purposes or callings. You can be assertive and strong-willed and still be sensitive. As you might already know, you do not have to surrender your warrior energy to be sensitive. You can possess both. People in the banana peel sensitivity category are living proof!

Examples of people in the banana-peel sensitivity category in pop culture might include Maggie Smith's Dowager Countess character from *Downton Abbey*, US Senator John McCain, artist/businessman Jay Z, philanthropist/mogul Bill Gates, comedian/cancer survivor Tig Notaro, and actor/comedian/author Whoopi Goldberg.

In conclusion: You're in good company if you're a sensitive person. Some of the most famous artists, thinkers, and leaders were also highly sensitive. So you're not at all a rare breed, just a special and sometimes misunderstood one. All of these categories of sensitivity are equal in worth and have their own strengths and weaknesses. You might fall into one of these categories because of how you relate to your sensitivity, or simply because it is the way you are wired. Keep in mind that your sensitivity can change or bounce around between these categories over the course of your life and you may feel like you fit somewhere in between these categories. I mentioned famous people in our culture for each category not to try to put the folks in a box or pretend I understand them, but more as a fun way to help you recognize other very sensitive souls in the world!

3

GETTING TO KNOW YOUR SPIRITUAL GUIDANCE SQUAD

THERE ARE ALWAYS many angels in the room when I sit down to do a reading with a client. I think that's why both the client and I feel so good, so comforted, and so energized after a reading. We both just got a big shot of angel medicine!

Some of the angels who show up in readings are guardian angels who have been with the client since before they were born. Others are helper angels who've come to help the client with something specific happening in their lives. Many times an archangel or two will show up as well.

People can initially feel nervous about working with Spirit helpers from the other side. But most folks feel very safe and comfortable around angels. Remembering that angels are intensely loyal, hardworking, loving, and—most of all—nondenominational is important. Angels don't care what your spiritual beliefs are. They just want to be of assistance and play a bigger part in your life.

But angels are not the only Spirit helpers on your spiritual guidance squad. Ascended masters, spirit guides, loved ones who have passed over (this includes pets), and your own higher self are also available to give you guidance and act as your divine defense. The best defense is a good offense, and your spiritual guidance squad is very proactive.

In this chapter, I'll go over the members of your spiritual guidance squad and hopefully make you feel more comfortable and confident about communicating with them. If you read *Angel Insights*, you'll notice that I wrote about guardian angels, helper angels, and archangels in that book as well. However, all the information you'll receive in this book is new and should give you a fuller picture or broader perspective of angels. I've also included some mini-exercises to help you connect to your spiritual guidance squad.

Guardian Angels

We all have more than one guardian angel, and in my experience giving readings, it is very common for individuals to have three guardian angels, although this number can vary and become much higher, depending upon a person's life mission and challenges. The angels have also told me that there are so many angels assisting each individual human that they will sometimes just give me a few of my client's guardian angels' names so as not to overwhelm the client!

Angels have often given me images of the three fairy godmothers from the 1959 Disney film *Sleeping Beauty* when I am describing guardian angels to a client. Along with the fact that there are three fairy godmothers in that film, these characters are similar to guardian angels because they are all devoted to their charge, Princess Aurora, just like guardian angels are absolutely devoted to you. While some angels, like archangels and helper angels, will assist many people, guardian angels are yours alone.

Guardian angels each have distinct personalities, just like in *Sleeping Beauty*. They also have names. The guardian angels of my clients will tell me their names during sessions, or you can feel free to give your guardian angels names of your own. The value of names is that they make your guardian angels feel more real, so you will call on them more often.

It's no wonder I loved watching those sweet, kooky fairy godmothers float around in that movie when I was a kid! They were my favorite part of the film and I remember wishing I could have my own fairy godmothers. Now I know that we all do!

I can often get a sense of a guardian angel's personality just by touching into their energy, so I can tell my client "this guardian angel is very sensitive and shy" or "this guardian angel is very playful and fun-loving" or "this guardian angel is very humble and serious." One of my lead guardian angels, named Samantha, loves writing and spirituality and always seems to be deeply involved in my work, encouraging me to take my career as far as I can and make time for this aspect of my life. Samantha has obviously been helping a lot with the writing of this book, whereas some of my other guardian angels—like Sharon who loves to nurture—were not as involved, though they enhance my life in other ways.

Guardian angels make an appearance in readings for many reasons. They certainly want to reassure us that angels are watching over humans, and encourage us to ask for our guardian angels' help and look for their guidance.

Each guardian angel will often give me a message for the client. This message could be very detailed, like "Negotiate a better contract for yourself at work" or "Try to put $150 into your savings account every month." The message might be more general, like "Take better care of yourself" or "Spend more time in nature." Guardian angels whisper these messages into my mind via my clairaudience so I can then share them with my clients.

ANGEL EXERCISE:
Get a Message from Your Guardian Angels

A few things to keep in mind when trying to get guidance so the process is not so intimidating:

You can ask your angels about anything. You may decide you want a message about something specific, like a romantic relationship you're in, or you could just ask your guardian angels for a message about what they feel you most need to know right away. Ask for this message briefly in your thoughts, prayers, meditations, or journal.

Feel their message. You might receive your guardian angels' message as a feeling or gut instinct about an action or attitude you should take. You could also feel a nagging sense that you should take a certain path or action soon.

See their message. You could see your guardian angels' message as a sign or synchronicity that shows up in your life, like reading a book or seeing a movie about just what you're wrestling with. These can be helpful messages for you.

Hear their message. You might hear your guardian angels' message in the advice of a close friend or relative, or in the offhand remark of a stranger. Angels love to talk to you through the people you interact with every day.

Write their message. The dictionary defines automatic writing as "writing without conscious intention." Get your journal out and write at the top of the page: "A message from my guardian angels … " Then try to let your mind go blank and tune into what your angels would say if they were holding the pen.

Helper Angels

It is also common for a helper angel to come into one of my sessions. Helper angels are freelance angels who specialize in anything and everything, just like doctors often specialize. A healing helper angel who has been working with a client during their grieving process might come forward and make themselves known during a session. Or a helper angel who wants to work with the client on a specific aspect of their career, like how they handle relating to bosses and coworkers, will come forward and ask to be assigned to my client. Some of these helper angels have already been working with the client without the client's knowledge, and others are simply offering their services. The angels want me to add that these helper angels are "excitedly" offering their services, because they are thrilled that a client will use their free will and hire them.

ANGEL EXERCISE:
Hire a Helper Angel

This is actually *much* easier than the process it takes to hire a human for a job (although remember that angels are never a replacement for competent human assistance—just a compliment to it):

Briefly make the request in your thoughts, prayers, or journal. You could phrase your thought, prayer, or journal entry in the following way: "Spirit, I need a helper angel who can assist me with something specific."

Don't feel intimidated by the process. The angels are giving me a clairvoyant image of an old classifieds section in a newspaper. Simply asking for a helper angel to assist you is like placing an ad—one that will immediately be answered.

Explain exactly what you require. Perhaps you want help with confidence, managing a budget, finding a new job, improving your communication with your romantic partner, etc.

Watch for evidence of a helper angel on the job. Helper angels tend to work fast! So whether you are seeing new opportunities, a change in your circumstances, a change in attitude of those around you, or significant synchronicities and signs coming your way, helper angels get results.

Helper angels will also reveal their names to me during a session, or you can give yours nicknames. You also might hear the helper angel's name whispered into your mind, or have a name catch your eye when you see it on a billboard or in a book. Once you hire a helper angel you don't have to worry about renewing their contract—helper angels will stay with you until the objective is met and they are no longer needed, whether that takes days or years.

I've received powerful feedback from people who have hired helper angels on my recommendation and gotten quick, amazing results. They sold their homes in record time or even just got through the line at the DMV in record time! Of course, we cannot always get instant results from angels. Some things—like healing or finding a partner—can be more complex assignments. But rest assured that helper angels are competent and committed to helping you through any situation, no matter how long the process takes!

Archangels

Archangels—powerful entities who are like generals in the angel realm—will also step forward to offer their assistance during my Angel Readings. Clients might initially think, "Archangel Gabriel? Stepping forward to aid little old me? Surely there are bigger problems in the world." First, every problem in the world is important to Spirit. No detail, even the tiniest one, escapes Spirit's notice or concern. The angels are showing me a clairvoyant image of someone getting pricked on their skin with a tiny needle. Just like you feel the smallest prick on your skin, so does Spirit feel everything in this world. Second, it is partly because archangels are so powerful that they can help countless people at the same time. Guardian angels are only working on your behalf, and I get the sense that helper angels only volunteer their services if they are not currently "overbooked" (like human freelancers, this can happen to helper angels too). The angels tell me that while helper angels can juggle several clients, depending on how much each client requires, they have a finite amount of time and energy they can devote to humans. This is different than archangels, who are more limitless, or can take on as many projects as there are humans who need assistance.

An archangel can be working on a large scale in a war-torn land and also helping you create a healthier relationship with your mate. Healing is needed in both cases, and the fact that an archangel is helping you does not dilute the quality of their assistance to another. Archangels are very potent medicine. Archangels will sometimes assign themselves to you, or maybe have been keeping an eye on you since birth. I feel I have this sort of special relationship with Archangel Michael. He has told me that he always kept an eye on me because he knew I would need him one day. Also, I believe I was destined to do this work and Archangel Michael was part of Spirit's assistance for me, written into my soul contract. *Soul contract* is a term used to describe the agreements we made with Spirit and other souls before incarnating as a human, regarding what we would try to accomplish and experience on earth.

But even if you previously haven't felt a connection to an archangel, you can always call on an archangel to intervene on your behalf, and they will always answer that call. Archangels are excited and honored when you invite them to play a larger role in your life, because many people don't. Archangels do not always wait for a human to give them their cue to get involved, but if every human used their free will to call on an archangel, the world would be a better place and archangels could do a lot more good. Free will is mighty, and in some cases angels are bound by our free will, since humans are also powerful spiritual beings.

Archangels who show up consistently in my sessions with clients:

Any archangel can show up to help or be called upon by you, so don't feel limited to working only with the ones in this list:

Archangel Michael, who I call the "hardest-working angel in show business," is a big help in my sessions. Very often when I tell a client that Archangel Michael has come into the session and wants to help, my client will reply, "I love Archangel Michael! I call on him all the time." A warrior and protector with a tender, compassionate heart, Archangel Michael can show up when people need courage or when they need to feel like someone strong and capable has their back. Michael is also excellent at giving wise counsel, helping people speak up for themselves or stand their ground, energy clearing, motivating us to make positive changes, and encouraging us to set healthy emotional and energetic boundaries. Often at the end of the session, Michael will urge me to remind the client that he is helping or has volunteered to help. He is very eager to be of assistance! That's a warrior for you.

Archangel Ariel, another fiercely strong archangel, comes into sessions to tell female clients, "You are stronger than you know." Ariel loves to work with women, probably because her energy is traditionally thought of as feminine. Ariel is a bit of a tough-love angel, and encourages women who are facing challenges to stretch themselves and dig deep to tap into hidden reserves of stamina. While Michael can come in to carry people, Ariel comes into my sessions to pick women up and cheer them across the finish line. However, you can ask Ariel to do things for you, like help sales of your book, for example (yes, guilty as charged), which can produce amazing results. Ariel knows we cannot do it all on our own, and the energy she brings to any situation on your behalf is formidable.

Archangel Gabriel comes into a session to let me know that I have a sensitive male either as my client or as someone in my client's life. If the sensitive man or boy is the client's partner, child, or parent, it can be useful for Gabriel to alert us to this information so we can talk about how this sensitivity is affecting the client's loved one. Sensitive men have much in common, but they are all still unique, and how they deal with or manage their sensitivity can be extremely unique. Sensitive men reading this book might want to make Archangel Gabriel one of their go-to archangels!

Archangel Chamuel usually comes into one of my readings when a client has been unsettled by world events or the collective energy of their family or coworkers. Think of Chamuel as a soft, fuzzy pink blanket. You can wrap Chamuel around you like a blanket and use Chamuel as a buffer between your energy and that of the outside world. Chamuel also encourages us to decompress by spending time in nature or with animals and taking breaks from drama and the news. Chamuel can teach sensitive clients how to protect their nervous systems from harsh energy or overstimulation.

Archangel Raphael is known as the healing archangel, but in sessions with my clients, Raphael often reminds me that healing can be required not just on a physical level but also an emotional level. Archangel Raphael will volunteer to help a client through a challenging diagnosis or healing journey, not by directly healing the client, but by helping the client find the best health-care providers, supplements, and other resources. Archangel Raphael encourages us to look at any challenge—in our finances, our relationships, or our career—as a chance for healing. The angels have told me in sessions with clients that thinking of handling a challenge as "healing" something in your life (like healing your finances, for example) is very useful. Using the word *healing* will keep you from blaming, shaming, or judging yourself, attitudes that can actually keep you stuck in old negative patterns.

Archangel Jeremiel enters a session to inform me that my client is probably re-evaluating major areas of their life. The client might be coming up on a milestone birthday or just entering a new chapter or phase of their life. One of Jeremiel's specialties is conducting life reviews, which can happen here in this dimension or once we get to heaven. Jeremiel encourages people to reflect on the past and make conscious choices about what they want for the present and future. If you feel like you're going through big changes or are in a transition phase, call on Archangel Jeremiel to help you navigate this change and make sense of your current path.

Exercise:
Use Your Intuition to Pick an Archangel to Work With

Method 1: To use *clairaudience*, see if you can hear an archangel's name in your mind. If you hear "Michael," then that archangel probably wants to work with you right now.

Method 2: To use *claircognizance*, pick a number from one to six—look at the previous list and go with the first number that pops into your mind. If it was two, then that means you should work with Archangel Ariel (she supports men as well).

Method 3: To use *clairsentience*, look back over the names of the archangels I've listed here, but do not re-read the descriptions. Feel into each archangel name. Does one feel warmer, seem to have a stronger energy, or call to you? If so, that is your best archangel to work with now. (You can find a longer list of archangels in my book *Angel Insights*.)

Ascended Masters

Angels make up only a portion of your spiritual guidance squad—those entities in the dimension we call heaven who are helping you to navigate and make the most of your earthly sojourn. Ascended masters, like Mary and Buddha—who also show up regularly in my sessions with clients—can be with countless people at once, just like archangels. Clients occasionally express surprise that an archangel has entered their session, but clients can feel straight-up shock when I announce something like, "Jesus is coming in and wants to say something about this," or "Buddha wants to work with you."

Often an ascended master has been helping behind the scenes without the client's knowledge. You can by all means call on ascended masters for assistance, but many times they do not wait for an invitation and come of their own accord. This shock a client might feel about getting a personal message from Jesus, for example, is less about not understanding that Jesus can be with many people at once and more about what the angels tell me is a "conditioned lack of self-worth."

This phrase is quite interesting, especially the term *conditioned*. Subconsciously, many people feel like they don't deserve Jesus's or Buddha's or Rumi's or Freya's or Ganesha's direct attention. This goes back to the notion of "sinners," and how in some societies and cultures and religions, we get conned into believing we are not enough. The angels are not pointing out this "con" to try to blame, punish, shame, or judge anyone. They point it out for two reasons. One, to let you know that this low self-worth is not your fault. Humans can be very hard on themselves, so the angels don't want this low self-worth to feel like one more thing you perceive as "wrong" with you or a "failing." Second, this low self-worth is rampant, so even if someone feels and seems like they possess a healthy sense of self-worth, there can be other narratives playing subconsciously that were instilled by the groupthink of a culture, religion, time period, or family.

The angels love to remind us that we are each special and infinitely worthy. They are showing me a picture of a copper plate that has become tarnished with time. The angels say that our infinitely worthy status never changes, no matter what we do or don't do, no matter how much wear and tear we see in a lifetime. Sometimes it is the tarnish that makes copper look interesting or pretty—or even that makes it more valuable. Regardless, the plate underneath is the same. The angels are also giving me an image of blades of grass. Even a single blade of grass is special and important in Spirit's eyes. You don't have to be the leader of a nation or in great crisis to deserve Spirit's attention. The angels say that we all naturally command Spirit's attention because we are so lovely, unique, and important. Again, humans, like angels, are powerful spiritual beings. Therefore, ascended masters are here to support each one of us at any time. Calling on them to help is one way to gain their assistance, but just thinking about them will help you embody their energy. The two ascended masters who show up most often in my readings with clients are Mary and Buddha.

Mary

Mary, also known as the Queen of Angels, is not just for Catholics. Like angels, Mary is nondenominational. She seems to come in for clients who are going through a temporarily challenging time. But as we all know, a temporary challenge can possibly mean months or even years (and can feel like forever until we are on the other side). Mary seems to come in for people with issues that take longer to resolve, to help these folks shore up their own resolve. Mary sits with people and brings them comfort, helping them see the big picture. This includes the idea of putting our challenges in perspective so they don't become so overwhelming, but also looking at our challenges from a spiritual perspective. The struggle or frustration you are experiencing now could help you be of more service to others one day, or set you up for a better, brighter future.

Mary's energy is loving, forgiving, and constant. Mary's love "stays the course" and urges you to do the same, no matter what you are facing. Just like she sat at the feet of her son, Jesus, when he was on the cross, Mary will stay by your side so you never feel alone.

People who embody Mary's energy: You might have had a very giving elementary school teacher or known a fantastic nurse or other caregiver like Mother Mary. For me, actress and activist Ashley Judd embodies Mary's strength and commitment to helping those in need. Ms. Judd has devoted much of her adult life to charity work and championing the underdog, traveling all over the world to do so. She used her 2011 memoir, *All That Is Bitter Is Sweet*, to call attention to children and women in need. She also helped expose the mistreatment of women in Hollywood and helped kick off the #metoo movement. As a woman of strong faith, she has said publicly that she believes there is mercy and forgiveness available to all. She's human, and flawsome (awesome in spite of and sometimes even because of her flaws), like the rest of us. But Ms. Judd has a passion for helping those in need, just like Mary.

Call on Mary when ...

You need comfort. Mary is a powerful nurturer and mothering energy, so she can soothe you during a tough time.

You need to stay the course. Sometimes in life we are carrying a heavy burden that we cannot yet put down. The angels have told me that Mary will "walk with you" during the more challenging parts of your earthly journey.

You need hope. If you are dealing with a scary health diagnosis, a big financial setback, or a romantic heartbreak, it can be difficult to imagine things getting better. Mary will give you glimpses into a brighter future down the road.

You need guidance on next steps. When a client is going through a very difficult time, the angels often give me the clairvoyant image of someone driving through a torrential downpour (sometimes it's our emotions, more than the circumstances, causing the intensity of the storm). I will see windshield wipers working overtime to wipe away the rain. Mary can be like those windshield wipers, giving you just enough clarity to take the next right step forward.

Buddha

Buddha usually comes into sessions to let clients know that Buddhist meditation might be something important for them to explore. Meditation can relieve anxiety and quiet a very active mind. I have noticed that many clients who are highly intellectual or highly sensitive have trouble quieting their minds and can experience racing thoughts. Buddha can also help clients detach from drama and their worry about outcomes, and might offer to work with clients to ground them into their bodies and this earthly plane. Even though Buddha is viewed as very earthly and grounded, he can also teach people to be in this world, but not of it. In other words, help us to realize that we are all spiritual beings simply visiting earth. Buddha shows us how to hold life at a healthy distance, or how to not become too attached. Buddha teaches us to be flexible about life and bend with the wind instead of staying rigid and breaking. This is probably why yoga makes people feel so calm and surrendered, because yoga teaches us to breathe and be flexible. I have observed that some clients are naturally more drawn to Buddha, either because his energy resonates with them or they have had a past life as a Buddhist monk or in a culture that identifies with Buddha.

Buddha's energy is even, grounded, peaceful, and detached in a healthy way. It is the energy of hard-earned wisdom and also the energy of witnessing or being able to look at situations from a more objective and philosophical perspective.

People who embody Buddha's energy: You might have a favorite yoga or meditation instructor who makes you feel more calm or grounded in their presence. For me, former US president Barack Obama embodies Buddha's energy. No matter what you think of his politics or policies, President Obama was excellent at never losing his cool.

Call on Buddha when ...

You want to look at something from a new angle. Buddha's detached energy can encourage you to step back and see things from a different perspective. Occasionally all you need to solve a problem or dramatically improve a situation is to look at it from a fresh angle.

You need to catch your breath. The modern world moves pretty fast, and life can get very full. Buddha reminds us to slow down and even pay attention to something as simple yet fundamental as our breathing. Mindful breathing can be a great stress reliever.

You're trying to rebound from a traumatic event. Buddha might inspire you to see traumatic events as not defining you but rather one of your soul's many experiences. I think Buddha is a great reminder of the cycles of life, that this human journey has its downs, but also has plenty of ups.

You need help quieting the mind. Buddha can help you get more comfortable and confident with traditional meditation, or encourage you to explore variations like breath work meditation, chanting meditation, movement meditation, walking meditation, or guided meditation. And don't forget to call on him when you want to practice quieting your mind any old time, like when grocery shopping or before going to bed.

You want to be less reactive. Buddha can help you not take the bait when someone you know does or says something triggering. Reacting to everything can be exhausting. Some fish we can just let swim by our nets.

You need to be more grounded in your earthly existence. Buddhism is a philosophy that is primarily concerned with the here and now. Not just the present moment, but this earthly chapter of your soul's story. And what could be more appropriate than focusing most of your attention on your earthly journey? After all, that is what your soul is up to at the moment!

Departed Loved Ones, Spirit Guides and More

Just when you think you've covered your bases with spiritual assistance, let's look at even more members of your squad.

Loved Ones Who've Passed On

Technically they are not angels, but departed loved ones can watch over us from heaven, send us guidance, and feel like angels in our lives. Departed loved ones sometimes make a guest appearance in a reading, especially if the client asks about the loved one during the session. Grandparents love to come into sessions, especially grandparents you never knew or were not necessarily close to. These grandparents seem to want to do "damage control" regarding family trauma, and help my clients understand some of the dysfunctional family heritage that might have affected how their parents raised them. Grandparents my client was close to or not close to often want to assure the client that they are still watching over and loving my client from heaven. It is common for me to suddenly be overcome with emotion when I make contact with a client's departed loved one!

Many times, loved ones whom clients never expected to show up in a reading do—often loved ones the client had a tumultuous relationship with when they were alive. These loved ones convey a strong sense of urgency about speaking to my client and making amends. Other times, souls might be embarrassed about things they did on earth and be shy about coming forward. Sometimes a loved one who passed early or "before their time" will tell me that they were not meant to be here for a "full" human life.

Many times these loved ones who died young had an energy while human that was very light and loving and so close to that of Spirit that they just naturally went back home. These souls usually touched, helped, and inspired many during their short lives. Other times the loved one might have almost burned too bright—been very adventurous, intense, outgoing, or reckless—and thus burned out on this life early. Or maybe they never felt like they fit in here and they abused drugs and alcohol to cope. No matter when someone passes, or whether their date of death was fated or more flexible, deceased loved ones always assure me that there is a reason for everything, even their death. They claim that this life all makes much more sense in heaven, or the dimension souls travel to when they leave this one.

People who pass over retain much of the same personality traits as they had on earth (if your Aunt Gladys was funny and sarcastic while alive, then odds are her soul still is). Although in my experience with departed loved ones in Angel Readings, people who pass over are much more enlightened, forgiving, and loving once their souls acclimate to the emotional climate of heaven, which softens people. Loved ones in heaven are at peace, but they can still feel regrets about their life: regrets about things they did not get to accomplish, regrets about the way they treated people.

I was told by one of these spirits during an Angel Reading with a client that departed loved ones can also be with many people at once, so they can have a front-row seat at all family events, even if they happen simultaneously.

If you would like to connect with someone in your life who has passed on, journaling is an excellent method. You can say things that were left unsaid, ask for or offer forgiveness, and tell your departed loved one that you'd like a sign from them.

Spirit Guides

When humans pass over and decide to remain in heaven before possibly reincarnating again, these souls often choose to act as spirit guides to a few humans still plugging away on earth. After all, who better than a human who has passed over to understand and be sympathetic to the complexities of life on earth!

You surely have a spirit guide or two on your spiritual guidance squad. Your spirit guides could be people you knew in this lifetime, souls who were important to you in past lifetimes, or souls you have never met before who want to mentor you or have something in common with you. Sometimes spirit guides are assigned to us before birth; others show up at appropriate times during our lives.

Spirit guides who were once human can offer advice, and in some cases can lend you a bit of their talent, courage, or chutzpah. You may invite a departed soul to be your spirit guide or they might volunteer to be on your team without your knowledge. You might be a performer and have a departed and possibly famous artist on your squad!

I've found that it is not uncommon for Native American spirit guides to show up in my readings with clients who live in the US or Canada. I do have Native American ancestry (my great-great-grandmother was full-blooded Cherokee), but most of my clients do not (and even mine was from way, way back). Perhaps these guides are showing up because Americans and Canadians are living on the soil that originally belonged to these people. When I asked the angels about it, they said that Western society has largely lost touch with both ritual and connection to the earth, and that these Native American spirit guides are trying to help us get that back.

Ghosts

What I like to term "lost souls" or "wandering spirits" are not a part of your spiritual guidance squad, but you might sense their energy, especially if you live in an old house or visit an area where something traumatic happened. Sometimes you are sensing not a true spirit, but just the leftover energetic residue of someone who has now passed over to heaven. You might even see a ghost (this happened to me once) who looks just like a human or you might think you see something out of the corner of your eye, and when you turn to get a better look, nothing is there.

I have worked with clients who had ghosts in their homes (usually but not always a former resident of the home), and helped them move these souls onto the light and heaven, where I feel they belong and are happier. Once a client told me that he thought there was a presence in his attic. "I went up there three times last month and burned sage," he told me, "and I kept thinking, 'Get out of my house!'" Meeting these souls with an attitude of hostility is absolutely the wrong approach and can increase any unwanted psychic phenomenon you are experiencing in the house. I advised the client to immediately switch tactics, and use a detached yet loving energy as well as call on angels to help, which produced much better results!

While you should not pay a ghost a lot of attention, which might accidentally encourage behavior like switching lights off and on, you need to have a *loving* or sympathetic attitude toward this entity. The next step is calling in some helper angels to help win this spirit's trust and escort it on to heaven. I speak from experience working with clients that this is possible, even with a ghost that has been in a home or with a family for decades. The angels and I successfully moved a ghost on to heaven who had been in a family home for over three decades and was wreaking some havoc and causing anxiety for the sensitive people in the house. I learned from the angels that this soul had led a tortured life, trusted no one, and was scared and confused. The paranormal activity was all about this soul lashing out. It took a few months, but when the soul left the home after the angels won his trust, I received messages of gratitude from that ghost and the homeowners. This very active ghost never made another appearance in the family's home and is now in a much better place.

If you have a loved one who has passed on, don't worry. Most souls go straight to heaven. Occasionally, though, people are scared to leave the earth plane or simply do not wish to or are confused and end up accidentally hanging around longer than they should.

Animal Spirit Guides

Animals can take on the role of spirit guide. If you encounter an animal often in nature or art, or often dream about the same animal, this animal is acting as a spirit guide and has some lessons or messages for you. Animals show up in my Angel Readings with clients, whether the animals are spirit guides or former pets or both! Before I get on the phone with a client, I always ask the angels to give me one or two spirit animals that could help teach my client a lesson about whatever is going on in their life at the moment.

Some of the most common spirit animals that show up in my readings:

Butterfly: A symbol of transformation, the butterfly comes into a session to let a client know that they are going through a major life transition. We all go through many transformations in our lives and some of them are dramatic and significant, almost as if we are birthed into a new version of ourselves.

Dog: If a client is talking about a relative and I see the dog around this family member, it means this person is loyal, steadfast, and responsible. The dog spirit animal can also warn a client that they are being loyal to a fault and not getting their own needs met.

Dolphin: Extremely intelligent creatures, the angels may give me a clairvoyant image of a dolphin during a reading to let me know that my client is smarter than they give themselves credit for. Dolphins encourage clients to be more playful. They're also a symbol of soul mates. If I'm discussing my client's marriage and I see a dolphin, it can mean that their current partner is a true soul mate. If the client is single and I see a dolphin, it means they are wanting a soul mate or that one is already on their way.

Eagle: Perspective, perspective, perspective! That is what the eagle tries to give clients in a reading. Looking at a situation more objectively or from a higher vantage point can be key to resolving a challenge. The eagle also encourages clients to view a challenge from a spiritual perspective, asking, "What is the spiritual lesson here?" or "Why did your soul have this experience?"

Fox: Have you heard of the phrase "to outfox someone"? The fox is thought to be an agile and quick-thinking strategist, probably because they have had to outwit hunters and hounds for so long. When the fox comes into a reading with a client, I know the client needs to outfox something. Maybe an outdated system at work does not give them enough flexibility or creative freedom. Or perhaps they have a health concern that they can outfox with diet and lifestyle changes or a different treatment plan.

Horse: These gorgeous creatures are highly sensitive, so the horse spirit animal can let me know that my client is highly sensitive as well. Horses can also show up if the client is craving more freedom, like a horse galloping across an open field. If the client is feeling very trapped and stifled, I might see a horse bucking against the door of its stall.

Kangaroo: It's all about the pouch, that safe, snug place where mama kangaroos keep their babies. When I hear the word "kangaroo" clairaudiently in my mind before I get on the phone with a client, the angels are letting me know the client needs to be nurtured and take better care of themselves.

Lion: If I receive a clairvoyant image of a lion lounging on all fours, tapping its tail, I know this means the client needs to find time to rest. Fierce hunters, lions know when to be in motion and when to take a break. They remind us that taking a break is not lazy, but practical and natural. The lion, known as the king of the jungle, can also encourage a client to own or claim their power. All the lion has to do is make their presence known to command this power—no other exertion is necessary.

Nightingale: This songbird flying into my mind during a reading might indicate that the client needs to speak up more for their needs, or it could mean that the client perseveres in dark times, just as the nightingale keeps singing through the darkness. I find that this spirit animal often symbolizes expressing our emotions about a difficult subject or to someone we find it difficult to be fully open with.

Rabbit: We always think of rabbits as being twitchy and nervous, so this spirit animal will show up to warn a sensitive client that they might be too stressed out. Occasionally I will see a clairvoyant image of a rabbit tapping its foot on the ground like the Disney character Thumper. This means the client is being too impatient.

Spider: This animal emphasizes the importance of careful strategy and determined action steps, as the spider takes great care to spin its intricate web. If a client is trying to make a big career change or plan for retirement, the spider can inspire them to be methodical in their planning and take consistent action steps. If one web is wiped out by the weather or some other disaster, the spider begins again.

Unicorn: A creature of myth and legend, the unicorn can come into a session to remind a client that they are unique or special. Often the unicorn indicates that someone has a unique purpose or life path, which will involve them taking the road less traveled or facing some unusual obstacles. Unicorns encourage us to celebrate what makes us different.

Wolf: Once when I was feeling very vulnerable I experienced a vision of myself in the woods with two large wolves at my side. It made me feel more protected and made me realize that it was time to be cunning about my choices and the way I took care of myself. Wolves are a symbol of getting our needs met. This could be true whether they are survival needs or simply putting ourselves first and maybe saying no to a friend so you can have some alone time or saying no to a relative who wants you to take an expensive trip with them, because you need to save money.

Spirit

Don't forget that Spirit itself is on your guidance squad! No matter how you define Spirit—God, the universe, nature—there is something larger than all the above-mentioned entities (angels, spirit guides, etc.) that is at work in our lives. You might think of Spirit as the intricate fabric of energy that runs through all life or the collective unconscious that every soul is part of or a sort of spiritual source—like the mouth of a river that all things spring from. This *enormous* Spirit is part of everything and is always supporting you. Amazingly, Spirit can sense even the most subtle changes in your life—your needs, your desires, your moods. I have been told by the angels that the best way to harness this energy or force or entity we call Spirit is to honor it by being good to each other, animals, and the earth. Since Spirit is part of everything, we should see everything—every child, every flower, every fish in the sea—as sacred. All these things are reflections of Spirit and its essence.

You might be aware that some people or religions believe we should not pray directly to angels. The reason I feel this is an unnecessary restriction is twofold. First, it makes people feel that praying is complicated or has a bunch of rules. This, in my mind, is not so, and makes people intimidated about speaking to Spirit and the angels, fearing they might do it "wrong." Second, I believe that Spirit misses nothing. Every prayer to an angel is heard by Spirit. When you pray to an angel you can rest assured that Spirit has been "blind copied" on the message! That said, you should always feel welcome to address your prayers or wishes or meditations straight to Spirit, whose love for you is infinite and unconditional. Like a thirst that can never be quenched, Spirit cannot get enough of you! So as much as I emphasize angels, know that Spirit is very present and active in your life and on your spiritual guidance squad.

Sometimes in my personal life or in a session with a client I will tune in to see where a clairaudient message came from and I will sense the magnificent energy of Spirit itself, feeling that Spirit was talking to me. Spirit does this more often than we realize, even via nature—like through the blossoms on a rose bush or the wind on our face. If you have been burned on the idea of God, you can always start by connecting with your angels. Through them you can heal and learn to trust your connection to Spirit. Trusting Spirit is also about trusting ourselves, as each one of us is separate from yet still part of Spirit.

Higher Self

Is it surprising to hear that *you* are one of the members on your spiritual guidance squad? The angels tell me that your own soul, or *higher self*, is actually the most crucial member of your squad. *Higher self* is a phrase you might have heard thrown around in spiritual circles, and you may have found it confusing. After all, who is this doppelganger claiming to be your higher self? Is your higher self making out with your partner or dipping into your savings when you're not looking? And if you have a higher self, does that mean you are somehow less or lower?

The first thing to understand is that your higher self is an aspect of you that is extremely wise and connected to Spirit. So your higher self is part of you … yet it is also separate from you, in the same way that Spirit or God or the universe is part of you but separate from you. The world of the Divine is more about "yes, and" than "either, or."

Your higher self can see beyond the surface meanings of things and easily access the big picture (and I mean the *really* big picture—like past lives you've had and specific things you are on earth in this lifetime to accomplish). That's because your higher self is not attached to this life as much as you are. Your higher self is more of an "observer," while your human self is down here doing the grunt work—getting your heart broken, taking risks, worrying about the rent. The fact that your higher self is more detached is part of why it's wiser.

One of the best ways to align with your higher self's wisdom is through your intuition or sixth sense. And if your soul is the most crucial member of your squad, it's probably good to get in the habit of connecting with this part of yourself more often. "What does my heart say?" or "What does my heart want?" are popular questions in today's culture, when we are trying to teach people to be more emotionally intelligent and get in touch with their energetic hearts. In addition, you might also get your soul's take on a situation. The best word to describe your soul, by far, is *expansive*. Answers or advice from your soul will, again, be big-picture advice that take everything into account, and in soul language "everything" can be a lot—your highest good, as well as the highest good of everyone involved in a situation. Soul guidance will also be more emotionally detached. That does not mean your soul is cold, but rather that it can rise above intense, conflicting emotions and see the forest for the trees. Of course your soul does experience and express pain, but I feel like the soul has an easier time of putting things in perspective once the tears are dry.

ANGEL EXERCISE:
Getting Advice from Your Higher Self

For this exercise, you will only need a journal and a quiet place where you can sit undisturbed. The goal is to get you in the practice of asking your soul or higher self for advice. Not only can your higher self help you make decisions, but it can also help you see the big picture of whatever situation or relationship you're in.

Read each question silently, and then try to let your thinking mind be still or blank (picturing a still pond helps me) while you wait to hear an answer from your soul. Answers could come as an aha thought, gut instinct, voice, picture in your mind, or a knowing. When you receive an answer, write it down in your journal. Remember that your heart is connected to your soul or higher self, but usually your soul can put emotions into perspective.

1. Where is divine timing a major factor in my life right now, either because something was brought to me sooner than I felt ready for it or because I feel frustrated waiting for something I have wanted for a while?

2. Where or with whom might I soften my approach?

3. What recently entered my life that is part of the big plan for my soul in this lifetime?

4. What am I longing for or desiring that would not be for my highest good?

5. What am I avoiding in my life right now that is more important or serious than I realize?

6. Who or what is waiting for me to make the first move?

7. What have I been curious about or interested in lately that is actually a nudge from my soul?

8. What are some of my callings or things I'm meant to do here on earth?

9. Which relationships in my life have great potential on a soul level?

10. What friend, loved one, or coworker might I be more mindful of or spend more time with because their soul would benefit from some extra TLC?

11. What was the deeper meaning, in a big picture sense, of a loss I experienced that has been difficult to get over?

12. Was there a silver lining or blessing in disguise to this loss, no matter how small, that could help in my healing?

13. What can I do to help myself heal and move on from this loss?

14. Who or what in my life is trying desperately to get my attention?

15. What have I waited long enough to take action on?

16. What will I have to wait a while longer before going forward with?

17. What or who do I need to take less seriously or put into perspective?

18. Who shines the brightest in my life right now?

19. What activities are the most rejuvenating for my soul right now?

20. Who or what do I need to try to make peace with on a soul level?

21. What do I need to stop judging myself for?

22. What do I need to ask for or speak up about?

23. What mistake or regret from the past am I holding onto that is actually holding me back by keeping me trapped in a past emotion or mindset or experience?

24. Who is a good spiritual mentor or role model for me right now?

25. What are some things I need to do to improve my health?

26. Who or what creates unnecessary drama in my life?

27. Who or what feels like they are sucking me dry?

28. How can I better connect with and utilize my spiritual guidance squad?

29. What might be a healthy risk for me to take in the near future?

30. What can I do to begin preparing for this risk in both a practical and emotional sense?

31. Who do I care about more than I like to admit?

32. How can I take better care of myself?

33. How can I create more time and space for my soul priorities?

34. Where should I be spending more time and energy?

35. What should I be excited about regarding the future?

Teamwork!

Your spiritual guidance squad is a "team," so they are always working (and always working together) for your highest good. At any point if you want to touch base with your spiritual guidance squad and make a request of this counsel, you can address them as a whole. Assignments will be doled out to the entities best qualified or able to help! The angels just gave me a clairvoyant image of an A-list Hollywood actor. It might appear to outsiders that this actor is a one-man band, but in actuality there is a team of people behind the scenes supporting this actor—agents, publicists, trainers, coaches, writers, directors, spouse, etc.—who help this performer make the most of their career. Likewise, your spiritual guidance squad is continuously working behind the scenes to help you make the most of your earthly journey. And unlike that famous actor, you don't have to pay some of your support staff! Although a thank you is always appreciated, the angels tell me their jobs have their own rewards.

4

HOW ANGELS
CAN (AND CAN'T)
HELP US

MANY PEOPLE HAVE a cultural belief that angels are like genies in a bottle or beings that just go around granting wishes. Then, when someone does have a wish or even a desperate need that is not fulfilled, it can lead them to believe that angels aren't real after all.

The truth—as I understand it from working with clients, communicating with angels, and studying metaphysics—is much more complex and nuanced.. Sometimes angels can answer your prayers just the way you want or even bring you something much better than your wildest imagination! Other times their wings are tied and they can simply help you do damage control, or might even bring you something that feels like the exact opposite of what you wanted.

In this chapter, we will explore some of these deeper questions about what angels can and can't help us with, and I hope find some answers and deepen your faith in the process. See how the information feels to you, if it resonates in your body and soul as true or if your intuition brings up answers and theories of your own. You also might have some memories pop up of times in your life that were similar to situations described in this chapter.

Rest assured that angels can *always* bring you grace opportunities to help you achieve your dreams or better navigate a challenge or tragedy.

Actions, Consequences, and Grace

People like to think that everything is set and fixed: Who we will marry. When we will die. Whether we will get that job. When and if we will heal. There is a comfort to it, the type of comfort that comes with surety. Yet while some aspects of our lives are fated or fixed, life can also exist in the gray areas and be far more dynamic.

We have all heard of stories in which someone jumps into shallow water and breaks their neck or stumbles and falls from a great height. Yet we have also heard stories of people being saved by miraculous means in these same situations. How farmers have felt a pair of hands pull them from their equipment when they might have lost a limb or drowning people have had a stranger appear out of the blue and swim them to safety. Usually when the farmer turns around to thank the person who saved them or the swimmer on the beach turns to thank their rescuer, there is no one there. Angels do sometimes take on human form and save people this way. But what about the instances when angels don't save us or our loved ones? They might give us a warning, but angels do not always intervene in a dramatic way.

The angels tell me we are all loved and "treasured" equally. And we are all important—"vital"—without exception. Otherwise you would not exist at all. Angels want to save us all and spare us and our loved ones any pain and heartbreak. But sometimes their wings are tied, because angels—who are not really part of this dimension, just entities who have visas to visit—cannot always intervene as directly as they would like to. Just like a foreign traveler has certain restrictions about what they can and cannot do in the place they are visiting, so are angels bound by a set of rules, no matter how unfair this seems to us. Why some people are miraculously saved and others are not has to be examined and answered on a case-by-case basis.

But one significant factor is that the earth is a place where we learn actions and consequences. This fact is not meant to punish us and there is no judgment, because many times our actions are innocent or made with the best of intentions. But in the dimension we live in, every action has a reaction or consequence. At times, the best the angels can do is try to "soften" the reaction or consequence, to spare us somewhat and keep us on the path of our destiny. If you look back on your life, you will see clear instances when the angels did just that. One way the angels soften life's blows is through bringing us grace opportunities.

The Gift of Angelic Grace

Learning more about the concept of grace will help you better identify those grace moments when they do appear in your life, which will increase your feelings of gratitude and strengthen your connection to Spirit.

Grace helps you move to the next level in an area of your life, take advantage of an easy shortcut to one of your goals or dreams, or make a trying time smoother when an angel cannot—and maybe would not think it appropriate—to stop a tragedy, disappointment, or setback from happening. Let's look at some examples of grace in action when the chips are down.

Maybe you have been struggling with a disappointment and your partner clears their schedule to take you out for the afternoon. On a walk downtown you hear a street performer start to play one of your favorite songs. You feel like it's a synchronicity from your angels and it changes your mood completely. Or perhaps you are a hairstylist who is missing the grandma that passed away years before. You go into work on your grandmother's birthday, and it's a slow shift. A coworker randomly sends over one of his clients that he doesn't have time to squeeze in. The woman looks just like your grandmother! Once you get her in your chair you realize even her hair feels just like your grandmother's. You end up having a long heart-to-heart talk. (This actually happened to a friend of mine who is a hairstylist!) Or maybe you made a bad judgment call and got in trouble with the law. In the courtroom you are shown some kind of mercy—perhaps a much shorter sentence than is usual or your lawyer expected, or the opportunity to serve your sentence at home near your family. Maybe the facility you are sent to has a wise and compassionate chaplain who becomes a mentor and confidant.

When an angel brings grace into your life, it does have an unmistakable energetic signature. Watch for clairsentient cues that accompany grace, like the energy suddenly feeling more heavy or electric, time seeming to slow down, or chills all over your body.

Usually grace comes "out of the blue," which lets you know that divine intervention was involved. Grace is often surprising and completely unexpected.

Grace guidance happens when things come together or work out without your having to do much to facilitate. You don't have to earn it or ask for it, like getting hooked up with the perfect business opportunity through a mutual friend without having to audition or prove yourself. Others might say, "How in the world did you fall into that gig?" Grace is the answer. Or maybe you overhear while standing in the grocery line that your dream house down the street—the one you always fantasize about living in—is going on the market soon. You go and casually speak to the kind and elderly owner, who takes a shine to you. "Why don't you make me an offer?" he says. "That way I won't even have to hassle with putting this house on the market." Pretty soon you are living in your dream home. (That's another true story.) Grace can work miracles.

Often the only action step needed from you is to accept grace. Accept the help, the money, the date, the dress, the opportunity, the new house, the dream job, the mercy, the comfort. Remember that grace comes not just in the trying times but the good times too. No matter the current circumstances of your life—whether you find yourself on your knees or on top of the mountain—angelic grace is a constant.

Here are some tips for identifying grace at work in your life:

Grace moments can be tiny—like when you are in a rush and someone offers to let you cut in line at the store before you even think to ask. Or grace moments can be huge—like someone giving you a career opportunity before you are "ready for it on paper."

Grace requires us to get better at receiving and surrendering. This can be very challenging, especially if you identify as Type A, a go-getter, a survivor, a warrior, a nurturer, or a healer.

You always have access to grace, even if you feel you do not deserve it. In the angels' eyes and in spiritual truth, you are always worthy and forgiven. The more you can believe this, the more grace will flow to you. If you want to punish yourself, you will be less open to grace.

When tragedy strikes, angels work overtime and you will experience more grace opportunities to help balance the scales. It is one of the silver linings of challenges—watch for all the ways angels support you and bring both big and small unexpected blessings into your life. This is when angels truly shine!

Angel Exercise:
Opening to Grace

I've compiled questions you can ask yourself to discern if something that happened to you is grace carried into your life on angels' wings.

1. Does it seem like many things had to miraculously come together to make this happen?

2. Did you do little (or, more likely, nothing) to orchestrate the grace event or opportunity?

3. Were resources or people who had felt out of your reach before suddenly made available to you?

4. Did making this happen involve people you didn't know?

5. Were you shocked by this development?

6. Do you feel incredibly lucky or have a huge sense of gratitude?

7. Did you just "dodge a bullet" or get your "butt saved"?

8. Did a life-changing opportunity enter your life out of the blue?

9. Do you have to pinch yourself to make sure you're not dreaming?

10. Is this outcome better than you could have hoped for?

11. Does your good fortune suddenly feel humbling, making you want to be kinder or more helpful to others?

12. Was this resolution very easy for you, almost like it "fell into your lap"?

13. Did this help you take a jump "to the next level" in some area of your life?

14. After you sit on the situation for a few days or weeks, does it still feel like a mini miracle?

15. Does this development take a weight off your shoulders or make your life feel smoother, simpler, or easier?

16. Did this opportunity make you feel special, as if there really is someone up there who likes you?

17. Did this opportunity come into your life when you were really struggling?

18. Were you helped getting back on your feet after a challenge?

19. Did this experience make a tragedy less stressful?

20. Was your faith in Spirit or humanity restored?

21. Did this not necessarily change the course of events, but significantly soften the blow?

22. Did this seem to balance the scales in your life more, as if after something really negative happened, another event came along that was positive?

23. Did what happened feel merciful?

24. Was this the spoonful of sugar that helped the medicine (a tough life lesson or event) go down?

25. Even if what happened was relatively small and not terribly significant, did it still make a situation—or even an afternoon—markedly easier to deal with?

If you answered "yes" to any of these questions, you no doubt experienced angelic grace. That's because angelic grace is operating in your life much more often than you might realize. The more you get comfortable with grace moments or consider them "natural," the more grace you will be open to. That really means you will recognize grace opportunities more and be able to take advantage of them. It also means you will probably draw more grace to you. This is because you are aligning your energy with grace energy, and in an energetic sense, like tends to attract like. Being open to receiving and practicing surrender helps you align to angelic grace. Bring on the grace!

Free Will, Choice, and Action

Many people who read my books get very fired up when they realize how much the angels can offer and how we can all create a much closer relationship to angels so we receive more guidance and intervention. The most productive way you can engage with the angels to get more of their guidance and intervention or "good stuff" is this:

Step 1. Use your free will to communicate with angels when you need help—simply ask for their assistance in your thoughts, prayers, meditations, or journal.

Step 2. Watch, listen, feel, and open your mind for angels' advice and guidance.

Step 3. Act on the divine guidance you receive.

This three-step process is simple and phenomenally powerful. In a reading with a client I was once reminded by Archangel Michael that using our free will to ask the angels for help with something specific (our finances, health, love life, career, etc.) gives the angels more power or leeway to help us. But then Archangel Michael elaborated, telling me something I did not already know. He added that exercising our free will to ask angels for help is a signal to the angels and the universe that we are "open"… open to change, open to guidance, open to new people and opportunities. This is how our free will can open doors for us.

However, I would be remiss if I did not also offer readers some words of caution.

The angels are reminding me that very few things "fall into your lap" in this life. Yes, some people will win the lottery or have their soul mate literally knock on their door. But most of us have to do the work to begin or sustain a romantic relationship or get our finances on track. You will hear or read about stories of angels saving people in dramatic ways or bringing astounding miracles into their lives. Much more often, angels will give us guidance about action steps to take to create our own miracles (like starting a savings plan, seeking help for an addiction, or trying online dating or something else to put ourselves out there romantically). The angels are telling me that like the old saying about the horse, angels can lead us to water but we have to drink it.

Earth is very different from the dimension or reality we call heaven. This planet is a place of dense physical matter, and dense physical matter contains certain properties and laws that must, or should, be respected. Bodies and bills cannot be ignored, and magical thinking about such topics can be a recipe for heartbreak. If you are sick, either physically or emotionally, find a qualified health-care professional or professionals. If you are having legal problems, consult an attorney. Angels are never a substitute for competent humans. I always say, and have said in this book before, angels are instead a compliment to qualified human assistance.

As well as being a place of physical laws that are largely hard and fast and respected by the angel realm, earth is an excellent classroom. Sometimes allowing us to go through difficult times serves us best on a soul level, and other times I believe the angels are simply not allowed to intervene into our free will and the natural action-and-consequence cycle of this dimension. The angels are telling me now that they have to "choose their battles," and that deciding if they should intervene in a miraculous way, and if they even *can*, is a complex process that is not entirely up to them.

While it is helpful to think of earth as a classroom, I have noticed that modern spirituality hammers this concept home so regularly that I get clients saying, "Well, I know that [insert heartbreaking tragedy] was a lesson," all the time. The problem is that people sometimes will not want to "own" their complex emotions about the situation. Yes, it was a valuable lesson. But something can be a precious, necessary learning experience and also make you incredibly sad or angry. We should never use "earth as a classroom" as an excuse to distance ourselves from suffering or our own emotions. In the past, people with a lot of money and power believed that God chose them for this abundance, while the poor were sinners or people working off bad karma. We can go to great, ridiculous lengths to shield ourselves from feeling and absolving ourselves of the suffering on this planet.

There appears to be a limit to how many times angels can intervene in a situation, just as parents will find their limit with a wayward child and resort to tough love. If you keep making a poor or self-sabotaging choice, eventually you will have to learn your lesson the hard way, because you and the angels will have used up your get out of jail free cards. Angels can and always do try to soften the blows, so even in times of crisis you are extended grace and mercy. This is because you are not here to be punished. We get as many chances to heal or resolve a situation as we are willing to take. So if you have made many bad choices financially and are forced to learn a hard lesson, on the other side of that lesson will be opportunities to improve your finances. This is partially because that's when you'll be truly ready to improve them and make the most of these opportunities.

For people who are less fortunate than you, and maybe were not born into a society or home where there was enough love and resources, you are asked to be an earth angel. Some people are very strong in their earth angel energy and are always looking to help and be of service to those suffering or less fortunate. But we can all access this earth angel energy and do our share to make the world a better place for everyone. Part of being a powerful spiritual being who manifested on the earth plane is assuming some level of responsibility for this planet and its inhabitants. Don't look to Spirit to solve all the world's problems. As part of Spirit, that is what you are here to help with.

The angels are giving me the image of humans as athletes, running up a steep hill. The angels are right in our ear, encouraging us to keep going just like a coach would. We are never alone because our spiritual guidance squad is following our every move very closely. This is something they are never stopped from doing! Yet they can't always step in and do the work for us. This life is our race to run!

Why Can't Angels Stop
Terrible Things from Happening?

It is common for my clients, even first-time clients, to be brave and vulnerable enough to discuss their deepest childhood wounds with me. Usually I will pick up on the wound in a general sense before they even mention it. "Did your father drink heavily?" I might ask. "I'm getting an image of him storming around the house shouting, and all the kids are hiding." Or I might hear "sexually abused as a teenager" clairaudiently before I get on the phone with a client. The angels encourage us to examine these wounds, not to make us dig up old pain, but so we can recognize how these wounds are still affecting us now.

Yet it begs the question: Why are children born to folks in active addictions, emotionally stunted adults, or physically or sexually abusive people? The angels have told me there is no "easy" answer to this question and certainly no "good" one. Any answer would be incomplete. A vulnerable child being handed to an adult ill-equipped to be a parent just seems like a cruel, unfair punishment. I won't try to dignify or explain away these situations, though, yes, they can teach us lessons about forgiveness, compassion, and healing that can enable us to become more dynamic, sympathetic people and may even inspire us to become healers or help other vulnerable children. All I can tell you for certain, or what I believe with all my heart, is that despite the unthinkable pain that occurs on this planet, angels are real, they are good, and they are supporting us.

I once spoke to a client who was badly abused as a child. It went on for many years, until finally a family friend found the strength to blow the whistle on the situation. "Where were the angels?" my client asked me through tears. I love doing sessions over the phone. It's a very powerful way to tune into someone, and many psychics prefer phone sessions to face-to-face sessions. (In *Diary of a Psychic*, Sonia Choquette says that when she first began doing readings over the phone, she was shocked at the ease of it. She said, "I could do readings easily, maybe even more so than when a client was right in front of me because their emotional energy wasn't there to distract me.") But on this occasion, when a client was trying to make sense of painful childhood abuse, I so much wanted to reach out and hold her hand.

"That family friend who finally blew the whistle was your angel," I said.

When I have asked in the past where angels are during tragedy, I am always told that they are right there with us. They are influencing and intervening when they can, and if they cannot do those things, they are witnessing. Though it causes angels "excruciating pain" to watch violence and suffering, your angels would never let you face such peril alone.

Sometimes the most they can do is try to influence people to do the right thing. Beyond that, their control can be limited, and the angels tell me it is "frustrating as hell." I think that phrase is quite telling. What could be more like hell than watching an innocent child suffer and be limited in the ways you can intervene?

Much like Gandhi discarded his expensive suits and privileged life as an English barrister to suffer among his people, so do angels choose to suffer alongside us. They are showing me clairvoyant images of angels holding people in hospitals as they take their last breaths, angels sitting in the passenger seats of cars just before a fatal impact, angels soothing a hungry child as it cries out for nourishment, angels marching with activists for social justice and equality. Yet this dimension and this life really belong to humans. We are in the driver's seat, for better and sometimes worse.

Addressing how terrible things can happen if powerful, loving angels exist is the "elephant in the room," the angels say. Sometimes if folks cannot get a believable, tender answer to this question, personal or global tragedies can completely shut them down spiritually and destroy their faith. Angels can only do so much. They need you to pick up the slack. If you are worried about the environment, get involved in a peaceful protest and try to educate people about your concerns. If you hear of folks starving in a far-off land, get online and make a donation. If people are starving in your community, donate food. Then say a prayer that their suffering ends soon.

The angels assure me that there are people in your life right now whom you could be an angel to, maybe even a child who needs love and a positive influence in their life. Find out who you can serve, find out how, and start flapping your wings. The world and the angels need you!

Predicting Possibility

I have heard many psychics say that readings predict possibilities, and I never fully appreciated this statement until I began giving readings myself. Angels will always encourage us to go after something we want that is good for us and others—healing, romantic love, career success, world peace—even if it's not a sure bet, and even if the odds are stacked against us. Whether the desired outcome comes to pass or not is dependent on many things, some of which are outside forces not in our control—global, political, and financial influences, other people's free will, etc. So it's best to concentrate on what is in our control: the action steps we can take, the helpful people and professionals we can partner with, and the divine guidance we receive from our angels. That all falls under the umbrella of our own individual free will.

I sometimes prefer to give clients a percentage of something happening rather than a straight yes or no. The possibilities that angels predict about our careers, our relationships, and our finances are just that—possibilities. The angels are giving me the image of someone surfing on the ocean, and a wave forming. When you see an opportunity to heal, grow, shift perspective, be of service to others, or receive more abundance, paddle hard with your free will. No matter the outcome, you will experience some kind of a miracle if you simply try to go after your dreams. The angels tell me it may not be the miracle you expected or desired, but it will be a miracle nonetheless. Sometimes it's even better than you hoped! Our actions and decisions—those things that fall under our control via our free will—help determine our present and future. This is another perfect time for me to remind you that humans are powerful spiritual beings.

ANGEL EXERCISE:
Learning the Odds from the Angels

Have you ever wondered what your chances of success were regarding a certain situation? Maybe you are up for a big promotion ... but so are three other people in your office and only one will get the position. Or maybe you're in a relationship with someone who loves city life and all you want to do is settle down in a farmhouse in the country. You might wonder about the odds of one of you changing your mind, or maybe reaching a mutually joyful compromise. You can always ask the angels for your odds and they will give you the answer via your intuition.

Beyond Yes or No

It can be difficult for your intuition to give you a firm yes or no, because many situations have lots at play, like your free will, the free will of others, your soul contracts or agreements, and the current conditions in the larger world. Sometimes yes and no answers are available, but other times it's better to work with odds.

What are your odds in this situation? A powerful question to ask the angels, your own higher self, or a psychic you are having a session with is, "What are my chances of success?" The angels have told me you can get an idea of your odds of success in, for example, getting into a college you are applying for. Just feel into the situation, and then the angels advise that you break your odds into thirds. Do you get the feeling you have a 30 percent chance of being accepted to this school? A 60 percent chance? Or perhaps even a 90 percent chance? What I love about this system is that even if you have a 90 percent chance of success, which are great odds, the angels are still leaving a 10 percent variable for something like the college having an unusually high number of applications that year or you getting an even better offer from a different school.

If odds are low: Even if odds are low, you can still be surprised with a positive outcome. Once when I was younger I was very worried about something catastrophic happening in my life. My own intuition told me the odds were high for tragedy, and when I went to see a psychic she confirmed this and told me to brace myself for the worst. However, she also told me, "There is always hope, Tanya. I do not see this working out the way you want, but keep trying to turn this situation around." Guess what? The situation did turn around. I appreciated that the psychic had told me to prepare for the worst, but encouraged me to keep plugging away.

When the odds are 50/50: Often when a single client is in an exciting new relationship, I cannot always tell them if this person will become a lasting partner. But I can say, "This seems like something really worth pursuing. It has potential and I think you two were brought together for a reason." Once I had a client say in frustration, "Can't you just tell me if this person will become my life partner?" The reason I could not was because the client had not yet given the relationship a real chance. I was told by the angels that this client should spend the next six months opening up to the relationship by being more vulnerable and trying to be more relaxed and natural around this person (showing the true self). Because she had not done this already, the odds were still an even 50/50. If a married couple is fighting, the odds again might be 50/50 on divorce. Some factors at play are: if they go to counseling, if the wife owns her part in the dysfunction, if the husband realizes his childhood wounds are affecting his judgment, etc. Other times a soul contract between two people is over and the odds are almost 100 percent that the union is ending. Likewise, a male client might have just started dating someone, yet I sense a strong soul contract between these two men, written before birth, and the angels give me 100 percent odds that the new boyfriend will become a husband or long-term partner.

Predicting Death

I have heard many spiritually minded people say, "Well, we pick ahead of time how and when we will die." This type of statement is usually said in a very dismissive way, like, "What are you gonna do?" It's as if our deaths are written in stone. After giving so many intuitive readings, I personally have to disagree. Sometimes people are taken when they are young or "before their time" and I believe, and am told by the angels in a session, that it was preplanned. Other times I think it is not so cut and dry.

I once gave a reading to someone who was struggling with a disease. Before the reading I got several messages from the angels that this client would probably pass soon. During the session, the angels told the client it was time to "hope for the best and prepare for the worst." But the main message of the reading was to keep fighting! The angels gave me the image of a clipboard with names on it, and told me that the client's name was not there. This meant that sometimes our number comes up, as they say, and it really is our time to go. The angels said it wasn't necessarily time for this client to pass, so he should keep fighting and see if he could beat the disease, which was at that time very advanced.

Right now the angels are giving me an image of a crop in a field and saying that every crop has its own special time for harvest. For some people it works well with their destiny and soul contracts to have their day of death be fixed. For others, having more freedom and flexibility about when they come and go from this earth is ideal. I think we also have to remember that from the vantage point of heaven, death is no great tragedy. Our soul never dies, and we will all meet again. That does not mean we don't experience profound, paralyzing grief when we are left behind here on earth, or that our loved ones, while fulfilled and happy in heaven, don't miss us or have regrets. I do think they miss us less though, because they can watch us go about our days, and send us love and guidance. And once you get to heaven you can see the "big picture."

What Angels CAN Do for You!

Now that we have grounded ourselves early on in this chapter by examining what angels *cannot* do for us and how we are partners in co-creating our lives here on earth, I'd like to talk about something really fun: what angels have to offer that you might not be aware of, or might not be taking full advantage of.

Angels give you comfort. Once a client told me, "I have never thought much about angels before, but I love the idea of a guardian angel watching over me!" I believe this statement pretty much sums up what most people think of when they think of guardian angels: comfort. It is nice to know that there is someone always looking out for you. People have told me that just the idea of angels makes them feel calmer, safer, and more confident. This is why some people love to have reminders of angels—like figurines or artwork—around their homes. I encourage you to think of your angels as protectors, buffers, constant companions, celestial life coaches, and Divine bodyguards, especially when you are going through a hard time and need extra support. When I became very ill fifteen years ago, with symptoms that were confusing, debilitating, and difficult to diagnose, the only thing that gave me the courage to go on was feeling sure that the universe was listening and supporting me. I could not have walked through that terror and uncertainty without the help of a very powerful force that I could actually feel by my side. Life can be very challenging, and you were meant to walk through it with powerful spiritual support.

Angels remind you of your worth. The angels tell me that another common reason humans like the idea of guardian angels watching over us is because it makes us feel "special." More specifically, guardian angels make humans feel important, worthy, and unique. The truth is we are all special and equally important. That is why, the angels say, it is so crucial that all people and animals are treated fairly and humanely. This knowledge that you are special should inspire you to lead a full life—go after your dreams, take healthy risks, use your talents, be of service to others, take good care of yourself, do your part to heal the planet, do what brings you joy, and fulfill your destiny. You deserve the best—that's why you were born with angels.

Angels shine a light on your path. Angels show us the next best steps on our earthly journey. When our soul comes to earth and takes on material form, our intellectual self forgets most of the plans and schemes and promises we made in heaven, although the heart remembers. So if your heart is calling you to a certain career, to be of service to someone, to love someone, to travel to a certain place, and so on, that feeling or yearning is worth paying close attention to. The heart stores the soul's memory. These memories are therefore not concrete facts likes names and dates, but rather memories stored in emotion. Sometimes we get the feeling we should do something at a certain time, like change careers or end a relationship, perhaps because our heart remembers that this was the soul's plan all along. Yet despite the heart's guidance, life can be very confusing, filled with lots of twists and turns, details and decisions. Some of these are not big destiny moments either, but situations that occur on the fly or unexpectedly.

Angels can always shine a light on the best course for you to plot. Not only do angels have access to the master plan of your life, as your heart does, but they can also see further into the future and further into the past. When you are confused or you are just about to make a decision—whether it's huge or minor—consult your angels in your journal, thoughts, meditations, or prayers. I often equate this earthly life to an old-fashioned sea voyage. And the angels are reminding me that back then every vessel had a navigator on board. Angels and your heart both act as navigators, able to shine the light on the route ahead so that you can navigate your life into its highest potential. Angels will shine a light onto the next best steps for you via any of the eleven magical ways that angels send you messages, which I will outline in the next chapter.

Angels offer you clarity. Angels can reveal a loved one's real motivations. For example, anger and lashing out might be a desperate cry for help if someone is typically strong and not comfortable being vulnerable. The next time you are confused by someone's actions or uncertain about their motivations, get quiet and ask the angels to shine a light on this situation. You will probably then get some aha ideas or gut instincts about what is really going on beneath the surface. You can also do this when you need some clarity about your own motivations! A reticence to start dating again may be less about a dislike of online dating and more about a subconscious drive to protect yourself from possible heartbreak.

Angels encourage you to be healthier. I am a huge proponent of partnering with qualified and experienced healthcare professionals, but you can also touch in with your angels about your health. Ask them what is holding you back from feeling your best. You might get an image of yourself bingeing on potato chips, or the next day you might feel strange reaching for your usual morning cup of caffeinated coffee (angels told me recently that sometimes living at our highest potential is not so much about what we bring into our lives as what we take out). You might hear the name of one of your doctors, get an image of yourself in a doctor's office, or experience a gut feeling that your hormones, thyroid, or something else is "off," which means you need to partner with a healthcare professional.

Angels offer you hope. The worst part about darkness like financial, health, or relationship troubles is that we can lose hope. The loss of hope is devastating for humans, and not just emotionally. Losing hope also has a devastating effect on our ability to change our circumstances for the better. The angels show me that when people lose hope, the energy around them is thick and grey, and that energy can actually make it harder for the universe to get through with guidance. This fog likewise makes it harder for humans to recognize guidance. When we are hopeful we are open, which makes our energy stronger, clearer, and more focused. This allows our natural energy to go out into the universe and attract things much more quickly. Therefore a loss of hope keeps us isolated emotionally, but can also cut us off from people and opportunities. Hope is like fuel, and when we have it we have the energetic tool we need to co-create our lives with Spirit and positively influence outcomes—even if what we get isn't always the outcome we wanted.

And let me emphasize that having hope does not mean we deny so-called "negative" or challenging emotions like sadness, anger, or fear. There has been a big push in modern spirituality to "suppress" these sometimes uncomfortable and inconvenient emotions and label them as unnecessary constructs of the "ego." Personally I think there is nothing more valuable or human or healthy or healing than sitting with and processing your emotions—all of them. You can feel terribly sad that you lost your partner, while still having hope that the future holds a lot of exciting blessings for you. Likewise, having hope does not mean ignoring inconvenient truths—like signs that you and your partner are growing apart.

If you are having trouble finding hope about a certain situation in your life, get quiet and ask your guardian angels to give you some ideas or send you some synchronicities to show you hope. The angels show me an image of an angel in a garden with a rake turning up new soil, or new hope, to sustain you. I suppose that is what hope really is—the belief that there is new soil or new opportunities, experiences, attitudes, and people available to us. Angels show me that they can also build a fire of hope inside you—just like building a campfire on a cold, dark night—so that you suddenly feel hopeful about a situation that had made you feel depressed before.

Angels call your attention to important people and opportunities. Has something or someone ever really gotten your attention and stuck out to you? It might be as big as feeling compelled to answer an ad for a job that feels out of your reach, or as small as a pair of shoes on sale that you cannot get out of your mind. Maybe you get the job and it changes your life. Or maybe you get the shoes and your partner goes gaga for the way you look in them. The angels tell me it's almost like they are floating above these influential, essential people and things, trying to get your attention. If someone or something feels important to you—whether it's a company, a workshop, a philosophy, a person, or simply a pair of cute heels, pay attention to that feeling. Angels can enhance the energy of these people and things so that, in an energetic sense, they become louder and harder to ignore. The angels say they can do this with you if you are on a date or job interview, for example, and the angels want the person you are with to recognize that you are important to them or a good fit for them.

Angels warn you. You might find yourself worrying about things you cannot control, spinning things around in your head, which is just annoying mind chatter. But other times you will get that "nagging" feeling. Like, "Did I turn off the oven?" or "Did I make sure to check in on my friend who is feeling blue?" Sometimes the angels will alert us to situations that need our help—like a friend of your child who could use some objective advice from an adult or a book that you are copyediting that is accidentally going to press with a typo in the first sentence (it happens). You might be at the doctor and get that nagging feeling about the results of one of the tests the doctor ran. That one test sticks out. You might need to ask the doctor more about those results or ask questions about the medication they recommended because of those results.

Angels strengthen your faith. Angels told me that they increase our faith by helping us see the best in people and restoring our faith in the world. Have you ever been really angry at someone? Maybe you were about to make a comment to them that you knew would be cutting and hurtful, or perhaps you were even planning to bad-mouth them at home or work. And then suddenly you looked at them and saw the vulnerability, the fear, the confusion. Maybe you remembered a good time you'd had together, saw their inner child peeking out, or perhaps a wave of mercy washed over you. Angels try to bring out the best in us so that we may bring out the best in others. This is really the definition of the phrase *saving grace*: when humans tap into their better nature and save themselves, save each other, and save the planet. If you ever feel like you've lost faith in humanity, the angels say the best way to get it back is for you to do something kind for someone, expecting nothing in return.

Unfortunately, to say that angels can do anything is not true. But angels can help with everything! There is always some "influence" the angels can exert over a situation, so go to them with your desires and concerns. It's what I like to refer to as the "angel assist," just like in basketball when one player can assist another in scoring points or in volleyball when one player will set the ball so someone else can spike it over the net.

5

RECOGNIZING ANGELIC GUIDANCE

Is it angelic guidance or wishful thinking? A client once asked me how often something we think is Divine wisdom is just our imagination. Before I had time to formulate my own response, the angels said quickly and clearly in my mind, "You get more signs than you realize."

On another occasion, someone asked me if angels have tough days. The angels told me yes, especially when angels give us guidance—like to choose a college major or career that is more suited to your goals than your parents'—but we engage in self-sabotaging behavior by ignoring or missing that guidance.

I asked the angels how many of these signs we ignore or don't recognize, and the angels told me the staggering figure of 80 percent. That means that over three-fourths of the guidance angels give humans is lost on us. Why? It could be one of three main reasons:

1. We have never been educated on how to recognize guidance and communicate with angels and the universe.

2. We are not present in the moment and not paying attention to our day-to-day existence.

3. We simply reject the guidance as wishful thinking or an inconvenient truth we don't want to see.

Since humans are powerful spiritual beings with free will, the angels will often respect our right not to listen to them. However, if the guidance is about something life-threatening or extremely important to your destiny and life path, the angels will "hit you over the head" with guidance! This can look like we're being forced into a corner by the universe for our own good. Or you might suddenly get so much guidance about something that it seems comical, as if you want to look around and say, "Okay, angels! I get the message." We all experience these moments. One or two of your own are probably popping into your mind.

It can be dramatic and painful when you look back and realize you could have avoided an unpleasant outcome if you had only listened to intuitive guidance you received but ignored or talked yourself out of at the time. "Why did I have to learn this lesson the hard way?" we ask ourselves.

In this chapter, we will discuss how angelic guidance can appear or the forms it can take, so that you can benefit from much more of the Divine wisdom designed specifically for you and avoid those crash landings!

We'll also talk about intuition, especially your unique intuitive makeup. Just as every individual is unique, I believe that we each possess a unique intuition.

Where Do You Fall on the Intuition Spectrum?

Intuition is the foundation or building block for communicating with angels and picking up on the signs they send. But don't worry, you do not have to be a professional psychic to communicate with angels and perceive their guidance. Every human is naturally intuitive and has a sixth sense. This rule also holds true for animals (who can be amazingly intuitive) and plants. There are variations in intuitive ability among humans, depending upon a few significant factors.

1. How much intuition are you wired for naturally?

2. Are you in touch with your intuition, comfortable with it, and respecting its guidance?

3. How much time have you spent reading about or studying intuition or psychic phenomena?

Let's start with the first variable: How much intuition are you wired for naturally? Intuitive ability will be more pronounced in some people. I was once giving an Angel Reading to a client who had several children. When I tuned into one of the client's middle children, the angels showed me an image of an oyster, but an oyster where the shell was removed, so the soft, smooth flesh of the oyster was exposed. I knew it was the angels' way of telling me that this child was incredibly intuitive and sensitive to Spirit. I sensed that the oldest child was also very intuitive, though not nearly as much as this exceptionally intuitive middle child. The youngest child, on the other hand, was not very intuitive. The youngest child possessed an innate intuition or sixth sense as we all do, but this child's natural intuition was diminutive. Interesting that all these children had the same parents and grew up in the same house, yet each child landed on a very different part of the intuition spectrum.

Intuition exists on a scale or spectrum. At one end are people who are highly psychic and easily employ several or all four clairs: clairaudience, clairvoyance, clairsentience, and claircognizance. Perhaps these exceptionally intuitive people noticed these gifts even in childhood, and could see spirits, hear voices, experience prophetic dreams, be very in tune with nature or animals, have visions, or just seem to know things. Ghosts and angels can be very real for these kids. These exceptionally intuitive and sensitive kids can also be very imaginative. So sometimes they could really be talking to an angel and sometimes it could just be their vivid imagination. These folks might grow up to be intuitives/psychics or energy healers, or any other profession under the sun.

The way the angels explained these exceptionally intuitive people to me, so that I could explain it to my client with the children who possessed varying degrees of intuitive ability, was via a metaphor involving windows. Everyone has a window into the Spirit world. The exceptionally intuitive people have a window into the Spirit world that is made of crystal-clear glass. In other words, there are no blinds or shades over this window … not even a thin, see-through curtain to obscure the view. These folks can sense the world of Spirit and communicate with that world easily and well.

On the other end of the intuition spectrum are people who have that "diminutive" sixth sense. The world of Spirit is not very real to these folks. They might go to church or other spiritual gatherings, but often they are going through the motions of faith out of a cultural or familial responsibility to their heritage. The world of Spirit just does not resonate with them or interest them. Often they don't rule out the world of Spirit or the supernatural/paranormal, and might even think it's a nice, comforting idea that there is another dimension like heaven. But the world of Spirit just isn't "tangible" or "immediate" to them. I also sense that these are, generally, folks who are not too curious about the world of Spirit, and probably would not pick up a book like the one you are reading! I think it's tempting for people to say that scientists or businesspeople, folks who are very grounded in the practicality of earthly life, would automatically fit into this category of diminutive intuition, but that is absolutely not so. The angel realm is reminding me that some of the most naturally intuitive people on the planet are scientific inventors and CEOs or financial professionals (whether these people consider themselves "spiritual" or not). From my own Angel Reading sessions with clients, I can assure you that highly intuitive people come from all walks of life.

When I asked Spirit and the angels to give me a visual metaphor for people with a naturally diminutive and in some cases dormant and unexplored/underdeveloped sixth sense (some people might be scared of their own strong intuition and try to deny it), the angels showed me a clairvoyant picture of a window with a black curtain over it. This image illustrates how much intuitive information these folks can recognize and receive—or are *willing* to recognize and receive—from the Spirit world. The answer from the angels is "not much." It's important to note that this diminutive intuition has nothing to do with a person's worth or intelligence. It may simply be the way they were wired and came into this lifetime—or the way they choose to live and interact with their intuition. While someone may not be wired to be an intuition rockstar, they are surely a rockstar in other categories.

I was very intuitive as a child. My brother was not highly intuitive, but he was great at sports—a natural athlete. It was a pleasure to watch him play, and I did so with joy and pride. Meanwhile, if you'd watched me play sports as a kid, you'd likely have covered your eyes with your hands and watched between a crack in your fingers! I was terrible at almost every sport. The point is that we all have different strengths and it doesn't make any of us better or worse than someone else. In spiritual truth, we are all unique geniuses, the angels say, with so much to offer. This "dormant" or naturally underdeveloped intuition can improve greatly if folks make the effort to work on or discover it. We can all dramatically improve our intuition by leaps and bounds through study and practice. Sometimes these folks will be using their intuition and not even realize it, making decisions based on feelings or gut instincts that they believe are coming from a more logical place.

The angels also suggest that a minority of people on this end of the spectrum could have a blackout shade over their intuition not because they are wired that way, but simply out of fear. Fear of communicating one-on-one with Spirit, fear of the unknown, fear of their own power and wisdom. Someone in their family or culture, the angels suggest, might have ridiculed or minimized the importance of intuition.

In the middle of these two opposite extremes—people who are exceptional and those who are diminutive in their natural intuitive ability—or at any point along this intuition spectrum, is where the rest of the human race can be located. The angels are telling me that "roughly half" or about "60 percent" of the population falls somewhere toward the middle of the intuition spectrum. If we go back to the example of my client's children, this client had a child who fell in the middle of this spectrum. People who fall toward the middle of this intuition scale are usually very clairsentient, meaning they get a lot of intuitive information through feelings. Clairsentience is the most common of the four clairs. People toward the center of the intuition spectrum probably get a fair amount of gut instincts, are sensitive to energy and other people's emotions, can read/absorb the energy of people and spaces, might be drawn to Reiki or other energy-healing work, and get physical cues from their intuition (like the hairs on their arms standing on end, chills, etc.). They are also usually open to and somewhat curious about the world of Spirit. The idea of Spirit and things we cannot always nail down or prove scientifically may resonate deeply to these folks, and I find that they are naturally curious spiritual seekers.

When I asked the angels for a picture that described these people's intuition—the ones who fall in the middle of the spectrum—I was shown a window without a curtain or shade, but the glass was not crystal clear, like with the folks who are exceptionally intuitive. This window to the world of Spirit was pebbled or frosted, like the glass people sometimes have on their shower doors: you can tell from the outside that someone is in the shower, but the image is distorted and lacking much detail. It is not crystal clear, but opaque. People with this type of intuition can sense Spirit, but they often cannot see or hear Spirit clearly. They may have instances of clairaudience (hearing intuitive guidance) or clairvoyance (visions as intuitive guidance), but these occurrences will usually be rare, whereas for the very intuitive person, this type of psychic phenomenon can be just another normal part of daily life. While some of these people might be naturally wired toward the middle of the spectrum, others could have high capacity for intuition, but—to continue the shower door metaphor—there is a film or fog covering their window to Spirit. This fog could be made up of poor self-care, fear of their abilities, cultural assumptions, lack of study and practice, and so on.

Why are some people more or less naturally intuitive than others? I think it's simply a matter of every soul being unique. I'm all thumbs at gardening, math, science, arts and crafts, cooking, sports, and many, many other things! Maybe none of those are crucial to my journey or what I came to earth to offer.

We Can All Improve Our Intuition— and Change Our Position on the Spectrum

Even though we all have varying degrees of natural intuition, the angels want you to know something crucial: Wherever you naturally fall—or currently fall—on that intuition spectrum, you can always improve your intuition, often by leaps and bounds, if you educate yourself on intuition in general and practice using your own. In *that sense, you can change your position on the intuition spectrum. If you want to.*

The angels are giving me an image of a car in a garage, a car that has been up on blocks and not used for years. This is how some people treat their intuition. Then I get the image of someone taking the vehicle off the blocks, opening up the hood, replacing some parts, cleaning it, putting in some TLC. Suddenly a car that wouldn't start or barely ran is cruising around the neighborhood. The more attention you pay to your intuition, and the more you read books like this one, the better it will run. This is why simply having one session with me can cause people to begin getting more intuitive hits on their own. My clients are "investing" in intuition, so they are getting a return. In a session, we can actually wake their intuition up.

For inspiration, the angels suggest that you think of something in your life you once were not very good at. Maybe finances, or dancing. But then you educated yourself, practiced, played with it, and suddenly you could hold your own quite nicely on a dance floor or with a bank statement. The same can happen with your intuition.

The way each person receives angelic guidance will differ, so if you are getting more feelings and aha ideas rather than hearing a voice, that's okay! Try not to be attached to getting one form of guidance. No means of communication is superior to another. All that matters is that the message gets through to you! We each get guidance in the form that's best for us as individuals. Your intuition could change or evolve over time or at different points in your life, enabling you to get more forms of guidance or use more of the clairs. Try not to get frustrated. Respect your own process and unique intuitive makeup.

Quiz:
Intuition Spectrum Locator

This fun, relaxed quiz should help you get an idea about where you currently fall on the intuition spectrum. I say *currently* because the angels strongly emphasize that you can improve your intuition significantly with study and practice.

It could be fun to take this quiz again a few years down the line to see how much your intuition has matured.

You can also do the quiz from the perspective of a child in your life. This might give you some insight as to the child's level of natural intuitive ability. It's extremely helpful for adults in the life of a sensitive and intuitive child to be aware of their special disposition.

All you need for this quiz is a piece of paper and something to write with to keep track of your answers. Answer (A) for "very often"; answer (B) for "sometimes"; and answer (C) for "hardly ever."

1. As a child, did you ever play with an imaginary friend?

2. Did you ever see or talk to ghosts or angels as a child? Do you now as an adult?

3. Was the idea of ghosts and angels always very plausible to you, so that you believed in these entities without having to be talked into it?

4. Do people seek you out for advice or someone to tell their troubles to and confide in?

5. Do you have clairaudient experiences, when you get divine guidance as a voice in your head that is not your own?

6. Do you get strong gut instincts—like feelings about people and opportunities—that later turn out to be correct?

7. Do you quickly follow the intuitive guidance you receive, whether it's about something small like which restaurant to eat dinner at or something big like changing your relationships or your career?

8. Have you had premonitions about yourself, loved ones, or the world at large that came true?

9. Do you have dreams about loved ones who have passed on or about angels?

10. Do you receive detailed information in dreams that could only come from your intuition or a Divine source?

11. Have you always been fascinated by intuition, and do you read books or take workshops on intuition?

12. Have you ever consulted an intuitive or psychic?

13. Have there been times in your life when your intuition took a big leap forward?

14. Do you use your intuition in your profession? (People of all walks of life, like health-care professionals, teachers, lawyers, financial advisors, and stay-at-home parents rely heavily on their intuition.)

15. Have you ever averted an unfortunate outcome by acting on intuitive guidance? (This could be something small, like getting the nudge to take a "backup" outfit to an out-of-town wedding, and then having the zip-

per on the dress you planned to wear break as you are getting ready to leave for the venue.)

16. Does your intuition play a key role in your everyday decision-making process?

17. Do you value advice from friends and family that seems like it came from their own intuition?

18. Do you receive clairvoyant guidance as images in your mind's eye?

19. Do you receive claircognizant guidance, or just seem to know the answer to complex questions quickly, like a download from heaven?

20. Are you known as someone at the office or at home who gets good hunches or comes up with unique, out-of-the-box ideas for problem-solving?

21. Have you ever had visions or dreams about past lives you might have led?

22. Do you always try to balance intuitive guidance with your own common sense and experiences in the world?

23. Do you believe that intuition can sometimes be "off" about future events, simply because larger forces in the world and individual human free will are always open to change?

24. Do you believe that the universe and angels are on your side and want to help? (Don't be afraid to answer

honestly here, even if your answer is "hardly ever."
If you answer "hardly ever," look for some signs this
week that the angels are trying to help you feel more
supported.)

25. Has anyone in your family ever been a professional
    psychic, or was anyone in your family known for hav-
    ing an uncanny and very accurate intuition?

26. Are you attracted to movies and books about people
    with psychic or paranormal abilities?

27. Would you say that intuition is one of your greatest
    strengths?

28. Do you regularly pick up on synchronicities or other
    signs from the universe?

Answer Key:

Natural-Born Mystic—*Most (or 18 or more) of your answers
were* (A):

You probably already knew this, but you are extremely
intuitive. You might be someone who embraces your exem-
plary intuition, and if so, your intuition will probably continue to grow and evolve over your lifetime, with results that
surprise and delight you. Provided you study intuition and
hone your superpower, you have the unique capacity to wow
people with your talent and become an intuition rockstar.

However, the angels are also reminding me that some
people who are very intuitive are afraid of this superpower,

or even wish they were "just like everyone else." Sometimes people who are naturally extremely intuitive can feel overwhelmed by genuine intuitive guidance, premonitions, or seeing ghosts. If that's the case, educate yourself about your intuitive experiences through books, and get advice from a trusted mental health counselor and possibly a professional psychic as well. Intuition is probably one of your biggest strengths in life, so use it—at work, at home, and anywhere else you find yourself—to help yourself and the world. Others may undervalue intuition, but you never should. It's one of your best allies.

Gifted with Heightened Intuition—*Most (or 18 or more) of your answers were* (B):

It's no shock you picked up a book like this one! You have probably always been attracted to spiritual and mystical philosophies. Perhaps you practice Pagan rituals or attend a church or other place of worship regularly. You might be a deep thinker or a deep feeler—and you're certainly a seeker. You have probably always felt a little special, a little more sensitive or tuned in to things beyond this world than other people around you are. Does the idea of improving your intuition to get more guidance and insight in your daily life excite you? If so, you are already open enough to improve and hone your intuition significantly. The moments of psychic phenomenon, synchronicity, and clear intuitive guidance you experience might be rare or moderate right now, but you are posed to have many more after reading this book and ones like it. Who knows how far up the intuition spectrum you can travel if you put your third eye to it!

Moderate Intuitive Ability and Tons of Potential— *Most (or 18 or more) of your answers were* (C):

Sometimes you could feel left out, wondering, "Why don't I get a dramatic dream premonition or even once hear an angel's voice in my ear?" Please believe that you definitely have a sixth sense, and it is stronger than many people's—I know that for a fact because you picked up this book! Your smarty-pants sixth sense drew you to it.

The angels are also reminding me that some people might find themselves in this category because they have successfully "blocked" much of their intuition. This can be for several reasons: You might have grown up in a household that did not honor intuition or made you believe it was something bad or silly; you might have had a dramatic intuitive experience that left you scared or confused and shut down your intuition; or perhaps you listened to people in popular culture who discounted intuition or psychic phenomena. Having difficulty processing challenging emotions or traumatic events can also block intuition. If you have not blocked your intuition, whether consciously or subconsciously, you might just need to pay more attention to it.

The angels have this advice: Start a journal and record any intuitive guidance you receive; make friends with your angels and ask them for guidance; act on intuitive guidance when it comes in; ask loved ones how they honor or listen to their intuition; look for synchronicities or meaningful coincidences that come your way; and read more books like this one (you can always go back and read this chapter again). Finally, get more in tune with your feelings. Clairsentience, or feeling intuitive information, is the most common of the four clairs. Once you practice calming the mind, being more present to the moment, and expressing all of your emotions (even the challenging ones), you will become more clairsentient. Above all, be patient with yourself and remember that simply by being human you have lots of intuitive potential!

Eleven Magical Ways that Angels Send You Guidance

A crucial step to successful angelic communication is familiarizing yourself with the most common ways that angels send humans guidance. These are the same methods that anyone on your spiritual guidance squad, including your higher self, can employ to send you guidance. We have already discussed the four clairs as ways that angels can send you messages. Here are some others:

1. Golden Opportunities

When I first started giving intuitive readings, I was approached by several people who didn't want to pay for a reading, but had something to barter. These folks were all well-meaning and offered what they were able, but I was discouraged. Then I quickly realized that these opportunities were sent by my angels: I had asked my angels for help finding clients and suddenly opportunities had appeared, although not quite how I'd anticipated (paying clients). Yet sure enough, for every reading I bartered, that person would tell their friends and family about me and how I helped them and suddenly I would have several new paying clients! You've probably encountered something similar. If you're hoping or praying for something and then an opportunity suddenly enters your life, don't discount this opportunity just because the package isn't exactly what you pictured. Stop and ask yourself, "Could this opportunity have been sent by an angel?" See what your intuition says!

When you make a request, angels send you what they have to work with as far as opportunities or what is available in the moment or the near future. One of the best ways angels can help you along your life path or destiny is to send you valuable opportunities to love, grow, be of service, and heal. Some of these opportunities will be in disguise and may appear on the surface to be unwelcome obstacles. If you need an opportunity in your career, your love life, your health, or your finances, don't be shy about asking the angels … and then keep your eyes peeled for what they send!

Action step: *Get out your journal and list some opportunities from your past that you feel were brought to you by Spirit. This is a great exercise if you've been having trouble feeling grateful lately.*

2. Musical Messages

Angels love to play DJ. Is there a song you find comforting to listen to when going through a major transition? If you start hearing that song out of the blue in stores or on the radio, it could be an angel letting you know that another big transition is on the horizon. Sometimes the lyrics or title of the song are the message. One afternoon I was about to give an Angel Reading to a client who was upset about a ghost, or "lost soul" as I call them, in her house. Right before the reading I turned on my internet radio to find some soothing background music, and instead of nature sounds, Cyndi Lauper's 1983 hit "Girls Just Want to Have Fun" came blaring out. I knew it was a message from the angels to have fun with this reading, to lighten the mood. The ghost meant this woman and her two female roommates no harm. During the reading, my client admitted that lately there had been a lack of fun in her house and her attitude.

Sometimes right before I get on the phone with a client a song will start playing—clearly and loudly—in my mind. It might be a song I love, like Fleetwood Mac's "You Make Loving Fun." If the client is having relationship problems, I know the angels' advice is for this couple to enjoy themselves more and remember why they fell in love in the first place. Other times I hear a song I had totally forgotten about, like The Five Stairsteps' 1970 classic "O-o-h Child." If the client has lost a loved one, this is a "promise" to the client that, like the song says, things will get easier.

If you are a music buff, the angels might start sending you music to help you get in touch with and express your emotions. And of course, angels will send you your favorite songs as a way to say, "Hey! We're with you!" Loved ones who have passed away can also use music to send you messages.

Action step: *Think of something that has been upsetting or frustrating you lately. What is the first issue that comes to mind? Now ask your angels to send you a song to help you deal with or better understand this issue. You might hear the song later today or later this week, in a store or on the radio.*

3. Single or Repetitive Synchronicities

Carl Jung, the famous psychiatrist and philosopher, defined synchronicity as a "meaningful coincidence." Sometimes these coincidences are repetitive. You might want to move from your current home, but dread the headache of finding a new house or apartment, packing up boxes, etc. Yet you begin to see moving vans parked on your block all the time and friends keep talking to you about buying real estate out of the blue. The angels tell me that humans can often be running on autopilot and these repetitive synchronicities are a great way for them to get our attention. Like a book on nutrition or meditation you keep hearing about from coworkers, reading about on social media, or seeing in bookstores. This book probably contains a message that you need to hear, and the synchronicity is like a clue on a treasure map.

Synchronicities can be one-off coincidences, like if you are on your way to a job interview, feeling nervous, and your sister just "happens" to call and get the unexpected opportunity to wish you well and calm your nerves. Synchronicities are proof that the universe is actually paying attention to your life and that you are a priority. The universe talks directly to us via these synchronicities, which are each hints that our dimension is more mysterious and magical than we realize!

Action step: *Start a section of your journal just for synchronicities. When you notice a significant one, jot it down. At the end of every week or month, go back and reflect on this guidance from your angels. Reflecting on guidance more than once helps the message sink in.*

4. The Ancient Wisdom of Oracle Cards

Fun, fun, fun! Did I mention these cards are fun? Inspired by and sometimes based on the tarot system, oracle cards are now becoming more popular. The first recorded use of tarot cards in Europe was in the early 1300s, but many believe their origins are broader and older. People have been using divination tools to receive guidance from Spirit since, no doubt, the beginning of "time." The angels are showing me an image of a primitive person in animal skins sitting around a fire, throwing rocks or sticks and looking at the way they land to interpret Spirit's will (these methods are still sometimes employed today). I rely mainly on my four clairs to get intuitive information during an Angel Reading with a client, but I like to use oracle cards for ten or fifteen minutes toward the end of a reading if time allows.

Oracle cards are a great way to give yourself a reading, and I do just that for myself every Sunday. I'm even working on designing my own oracle card deck.

Tips for Using Oracle Cards

Choose your deck mindfully. Before I get on the phone with a client to do a psychic reading, I ask my intuition which oracle card deck or decks I might use toward the end of the session. The deck I'm guided to use with each client tells me something about the client's personality or what they're struggling with. When purchasing decks, choose ones you feel particularly drawn to.

Treat your decks as sacred objects. Once I'm through using cards for a client or myself, I immediately put them back in a closed drawer. This protects a deck's energy by keeping it neutral and shows that you respect this tool.

You don't have to ask any special question or set an intention. Your intuition will always tell you what you need to know most at the time. I like to come to the cards with a blank, open mind. When reading for yourself, just make sure you're alone in a quiet place where you can tune into your own energy. If reading for someone else, just concentrate on the other person as you're shuffling the cards.

Find your shuffling method. Personally I like to shuffle the deck until a card sticks out dramatically or even flies out. Others might shuffle until they get a feeling to stop and pick the card on top of the deck at that moment. Play around with it. You can use a traditional tarot spread, like the Celtic cross, or the popular three-card spread, where one card represents the past, another the present, and the last the future. I like to simply ask my intuition how many cards to draw from a deck for a client. Many people enjoy picking one card each morning to set the tone or intention for the day.

Pay attention to your first intuitive hits as you pull each card. When I pull a card for a client, I will immediately get two to three intuitive messages about how this card relates specifically to my client. No matter what card you draw, you cannot go wrong if you use your own intuition to interpret what this card means just for you. That way you will always get a "right" message. Expect some of these intuitive insights to come as surprises—guidance you had never considered before. Go with your instincts and thoughts about what the card means, even if it does not quite match up with the card's printed message or the image. If you don't get a couple of immediate hits when looking at a card, sit with it calmly for a minute or two and see what floats to the surface, or move on to another card and come back later.

The images hold as much meaning as the words. Sometimes the words on a card won't resonate, but the picture of a man on the card will remind you of your father, or an animal will remind you of one of your pets. Cards with images of a particular season might be telling you that a career change or marriage proposal will come in the fall, for example.

5. **Dreams of Premonition, Warning, Wisdom, Past Lives, and Visitation**

Not only can you receive intuitive guidance from dreams, but angels, ascended masters, spirit guides, your higher self, and loved ones who have passed on can actually visit you in dreams! After my mother passed, she visited me in a dream while I was in college and told me I needed to end an unhealthy relationship. She had worked with computers in the 80s, back when they were enormous and spit out giant reams of paper. In the dream, she kept handing me computer paper that read, "If you tell them you don't love them, they will go away." When I woke up it took me a minute to interpret the dream, but then it gave me the courage to move on.

If you suspect that a dream was angelic guidance, a premonition, or in some way significant, grab your journal and write down as many details about the dream as you can remember as soon as you wake up. If you have these types of intuitive dreams regularly or even semi-regularly, keep a dream journal. You may have a premonition dream that you will fall pregnant at a certain time of year (in the dream you notice that your belly is large and that there is snow outside on the ground), and if you get pregnant it could be fun to look back at your journal and the details of this dream.

I have had important wisdom communicated to me about my career and even my health in dreams. This is information I had no knowledge of in waking life, and occasionally the information was given to me in terms I was unfamiliar with—names of supplements, names of books—that I had to look up after the dream.

Many people report having dreams of natural disasters or other catastrophes days before the events. In these cases, people are often picking up on what will happen in the future, as opposed to being given helpful information from their spiritual guidance squads. Often in these dreams there are not enough specific details for the person to warn anyone or help avert disaster. If you are meant to warn someone or you have a warning dream about your own life, you will be given enough details in the dream to take appropriate action.

You may have dreams about past lives. If you are dreaming and experience yourself in a different culture, time period, dress, or role, it could be a sort of past life flashback or memory, which perhaps holds significance regarding your current life. Try to figure out how this past life is particularly relevant to something going on in your current life—probably something you are struggling with, which is why you had the dream in the first place. Past life information can often come to us in waking visions. Sometimes waking visions will happen at night. These are not quite dreams, but perhaps something about our brains being just out of a sleeping state—like people who wake up in the middle of the night and report seeing an angel or a ghost in their room—facilitates these visions.

Action step: *If you are missing a loved one who passed, or are very confused about a situation in your life, ask the angels for guidance just before you lay your head on the pillow to go to sleep. If you do not have a dream, you still might wake up the next morning with more clarity or peace about the situation.*

6. People as Emissaries of Spirit

Angels speak to us through our loved ones, coworkers, or even the teller at our local bank, because it's often the most direct way to reach us. Because a human is speaking the message right to us, there is a better chance that we will hear angelic guidance loud and clear. The angels add that when you hear just the right words from someone in your life at just the right time, this message was divinely inspired. So angelic communication via friends and loved ones is not to be underestimated! You have certainly played the part of unwitting messenger, delivering angelic advice to others! This is one of our purposes, and we are all part-time employees of heaven.

A friend or loved one might have a great idea appear in their mind (claircognizance). Then they might announce, "Hey, I know what you should do about that problem at your office!"

Perhaps you keep coming back to this advice from a loved one, replaying it in your mind or having it suddenly pop into your mind. Sometimes friends and family can deliver an angel message that cuts through the fog. The fog can be confusion, fear, anxiety, hopelessness … any emotion that has you stuck. Often even the person relaying the message to you will get the intuitive sense that they have said something important, that this is advice you really need to hear. Or they might preface the message by saying something like, "I'm not sure why, but I feel I need to tell you this" or "I don't know how this came into my mind, but ..." or "This might seem out of the box, but ..."

Occasionally strangers will say amazingly insightful things to you in passing that are actually clues or signs from your spiritual guidance squad. You may have followed this insightful advice, or maybe you ignored it, only realizing years later how profound or appropriate the advice was.

Of course, sometimes friends and family can say exactly the *wrong* thing! Or they might give us well-meaning advice that just doesn't fit the situation. But when a friend, family member, coworker, health-care provider, acquaintance, or stranger says something that resonates deeply with you, seems to come out of left field, or you have a strong immediate reaction to—whether your reaction is negative or positive—pay close attention. This might really be a message from your angels, hand-delivered by a human.

Action step: *Keep your ears open this week for words of wisdom delivered by people in your life that could really be coming from your spiritual guidance squad, just like your mailperson delivers letters from someone else.*

7. Angel Numbers and Number Sequences

Finding significance in numbers and number sequences is an idea that dates back to ancient times, and numerology—the belief in a divine, mystical connection between numbers and events—is currently enjoying a resurgence in popularity. Studying Kabbalah, an ancient Jewish mystical tradition, taught me much about numbers and their meanings.

The angels love to show us number sequences that appear in threes. Although take note that while it's popular to talk about seeing 444, for example, seeing the number 4 alone or in a pair is also powerful and can be full of meaning. I have a client who sees a lot of "split" angel numbers. Instead of looking at a clock and seeing 1:11, he seems to glance at his phone at 11:41.

Angels are very aware of numbers that are significant just to you, and will send you those numbers as messages. If every apartment or home you've ever lived in contains the numbers 5 and 2 in its address, and a property manager shows you apartment #502, the angels are probably letting you know this is your next home. If you have a lucky number, also pay attention when it appears "randomly." Lately I have had clients say that they see a lot of number sequences that pop up again and again, but not ones that necessarily hold any particular significance. "What does it mean?" they ask. The angels have told me that this is their way of getting your attention and reminding you that the universe is always paying attention to you, because you are special.

Below are some common angel numbers—and their general meanings—that often appear in groups of three, and might get your attention on a license plate, in a phone number, on a bill, on a billboard, or anywhere else you see numbers. Numbers are everywhere, just like angels! You might also see these numbers in single form, which can still have great significance. However, the angels tell me that often angelic guidance is sent with numbers in groups, because that stands out and gets our attention, signaling to us that we are seeing something special.

111: This angel number has a powerful energy signature. If you happen to look up at the clock at 1:11, or a barista gives you $1.11 in change for your latte, the angels are telling you that now is a great moment for manifesting. Don't be alarmed if you see 111, or any angel number sequence, several times over the course of a day or week. Remember, angels are always trying to get our attention to give us guidance, and sometimes it feels like they really get in our faces about it!

At different times, the energy around us is more conducive to something in particular, and 111 is an indication that the energy around you right now is ripe for taking healthy risks, shifting patterns, or moving projects or relationships forward. The angels tell me that 111 can also be a reminder that you are co-creating your reality. 111 seems to be the most popular angel number and, along with 444, one that is seen the most often.

The next time you notice 111, stop and make a wish or set an intention! The energy around you is now heightened and receptive.

222: For a time I saw the number 222 everywhere! It almost became silly how often I noticed 222 on an electricity bill, on the price tag of clothing, or on a license plate. Because I was working hard to change my life and build something new, the angels placing this number in front of me often made perfect sense, because the message of 222 is about metaphorical farming. If you see this angel number, keep planting seeds (at your job, in a relationship, with your finances) and tending your burgeoning crop. Your efforts may not look like much now, but you are laying the groundwork for a substantial harvest in the future!

When you are wondering if you're on the right path in an area of your life, seeing 222 can be a welcome confirmation from the angels that you're headed in the right direction and should keep plugging. 222, the angels tell me, is a number of encouragement.

When you see 222, remember that some of the conditions of our present life might be the crop we are harvesting from seeds planted in the past. Think about what seeds you want to plant now with your health, finances, relationships, and career. This will positively affect your future harvest!

333: This is a number of prayers answered, a reminder that angels know what you want and what you are working toward, and that they are bringing those opportunities and resources into your life. 333 is also an invitation to go forward fearlessly, taking action steps toward your dreams and knowing that Spirit, the universe, and your angels have your back. I find this number encourages clients to believe that everything they need to accomplish their destiny, change their lives for the better, or get through a difficult time is somehow already out there waiting for them. This is how your prayers have already been answered!

The angel number 333 is an invitation to stop and reflect on the resources you have access to that can help you achieve a goal or get through a challenging time. Remember this metaphor: Angels will bring you all the timber and tools you need, but you must roll up your sleeves and build the house

444: The angels do have a favorite number sequence: 444. You might see 444 when you're going through a tough breakup, dealing with a difficult diagnosis, or feeling lonely. 444 is simply a reminder that angels are near and supporting you, and seeing this number when you're feeling low can be very comforting and reassuring. You could see 444 after a big win at the office, or while you're enjoying a dream vacation. Again, it's a reminder the angels are with you, and that they likely had a hand in helping the universe bring you these blessings! That is why 444 is also a number of grace and mercy, letting us know that there are some things we don't have to work for—they are just given to us. If an e-mail from a new client comes in at exactly 4:44, or you get off the phone with your crush and notice the clock reads exactly 4:44, take this as a good omen!

Think of seeing 444 as angels "winking" at you! The next time you see 444, wink back by saying a silent hello or prayer of thanks to your angels.

555: Now and then the number 555 will come into my premeditation before I get on the phone with a client for an Angel Reading. This angel number lets me know the client is going through a time of major transition with lots of changes. We all have seasons when it seems like everything is shifting in our life, as if we are having a super-charged growth spurt. Seeing 555 when things feel chaotic or unfamiliar is a grounding, calming reminder from the angels that transitions can be intense, even when we are experiencing changes we have longed for or worked very hard for.

Whatever transition you are going through, even if it seems negative on the surface—being fired, getting divorced, experiencing a healing crisis, moving to locations far away from loved ones—transitions are always a restructuring and reconfiguring of your soul's path and potential. Ultimately you will come out the other side much better for the experience.

When you see 555 during a time of challenges, reflect on something that is changing in your life, and seems to be changing for the worse. Try to find the blessing in disguise or silver lining of this situation, and imagine a way that this change may serve you in the long run.

666: The angels inform me that the number six is one of beauty, balance, and integrity. They also say that the number 666 simply means more of these magnificent things, and that we should never let anyone spook us into believing that a number has power or represents bad intentions. Numbers are simply a language. 666 has to do with earthly, material concerns, so you might see this number when you are worried about your career, home, or finances. It can also encourage you to bring more beauty and pleasure into your life.

This number can be a call or need for balance in all our affairs, and you might see it if you have a health concern that would benefit from you living a more balanced lifestyle or eating a more balanced diet. This is why 666 can also be a number of sacrifice or letting go of what is not serving us. You might encounter this number when you are experiencing a financial windfall, informing you that balance is in order—some of this money should be put away for a rainy day.

Encountering the angel number 666 can be a reminder of the healing, transformative power of beauty. Go buy a bunch of fresh, inexpensive flowers and notice how they transform your energy or the energy of a room.

777: An angel number about spirituality, you might encounter it during phases in life when you're focusing on or prioritizing your spirituality, learning about or incorporating new spiritual practices, or on the road of a seeker.

This number can also be a reminder that you should acknowledge the spiritual side of any work you are performing, since all work is a form of service and therefore offers something sacred. 777 can be a number you see when your spirituality is expanding and you're tapping into that deep well of spiritual awareness that exists in all of us.

When you see 777, ask yourself if there is a spiritual practice like meditation or a spiritual tradition like shamanism that you've been curious about. Get a book or listen to a podcast on the subject!

888: You might see the number 888, which signals abundance, on a check you receive for services performed, to let you know that there is the possibility of good financial abundance with this particular client, company, or simply the type of work you are currently doing. 888 can also be a hint from the angels that we each have access to the universe's abundance, and angels can help us bring more of that abundance into any area of our life—like romance, career, or health.

888 encourages you to stay open to abundance in whatever form it appears, not just the forms we expect or have become attached or "addicted" to. If you possess an abundance of anything—love, time, money—the angels say spread it around and that same abundance will "boomerang" back to you! In many spiritual traditions, 8 represents eternity.

One way to bring more abundance into your life is to acknowledge or concentrate on the abundance you already have. This is how we align ourselves to the energy of abundance and call more of it in.

999: Life is "cyclical," and the number 9 emphasizes that "all things end" or come to a "completion." You might see 999 or a split angel number like 909 on a license plate as you drive away from your high school or college graduation ceremony, reminding you that a chapter in your life is ending. It's no coincidence that it takes 9 months to grow a little baby in the human womb.

You might see the number 9 when you are struggling to complete a goal or when you are losing steam toward the end of a large project, reminding you that success or the finish line is right around the corner. 999 can also be a signal that you have come to the end of one phase of your life, and that you might consider what you'd like to do next. 999 can encourage you to let go of something that has run its course—like a job or relationship—when your soul contract with a person or institution has ended.

You may not be surprised if you've been seeing a lot of nines lately, as we often intuitively sense the ending of something before it has actually come. Sit with your journal and ponder some things that seem to be coming to an end in your life. It could be a role winding down or a self-sabotaging attitude or negative pattern that seems to be releasing.

8. Angel Nudges

Have you ever felt a nagging urge to do something, like smile at a stranger, call a friend out of the blue, launch a project ahead of the planned date, or turn down an opportunity that looked good on paper? These are all examples of angel nudges, when angels gently but consistently push you to do or not do something. An angel nudge can make you feel just like the princess felt in the famous fairy tale *The Princess and the Pea*—a little uncomfortable.

I've gotten familiar enough with angel nudges to heed them sooner rather than later. This is important, since angel nudges are there to make your life easier, help you help someone else, enable you to make better choices, or assist you in avoiding potholes on the road of life. So the next time you have some small, nagging feeling that won't let go, or you sense that something just isn't right—like when you have the feeling that you need to pose a question or reveal a symptom you're having to your doctor—pay attention to this nudge from the angels.

I find that while we do get angel nudges about large things—like making major changes in life related to career, health, relationships, or finances—more often we get small angel nudges every day. This could be an angel nudge to e-mail that client and give them some words of hope, to help out a colleague at work, to take the high road, to let someone else have the last word, to cool off before sharing your concerns with someone, to take that mean-spirited rant down from your social media page, to apologize about hurt words or a misunderstanding, to give yourself a break and slow down, to splurge, to save, to eat healthier, to hold off on something, or to push forward ASAP.

Action step: *What have the angels and your own intuition been nudging you to do or not do for the past few days or weeks? Heed the angel nudge now.*

9. Relationship Lessons

At times the best way for angels to give humans guidance is through one-on-one coaching. An excellent way to achieve this is to place a relationship in our lives that helps us learn, heal, or grow. These relationships might last our entire lives, but just as often, they are relationships that come and go or evolve. You might receive a diagnosis and then be introduced to a health-care professional who guides or shepherds you through the healing process. Once you are healed or the condition is manageable, this person may no longer play a starring role in your life. Or you might move on to a new healer who can teach you something different and fill in more missing pieces of your health puzzle.

Many times in readings I have heard people say, "I wish I had not married this person" or "I wish I had dated someone else instead." Yet often these romantic relationships that are not "forever" were fated, sent to help us shift, learn, and love in certain ways. Maybe they teach us what we don't want, trigger some of our deepest wounds and invite us to heal them (whether from this life or a past life), force us to become more independent and confident, or bring beautiful children or other family members into our lives.

A relationship with your boss could be something that was sent by the angels because this person is an ideal mentor for you, helping to shape the next decade of your career. Or maybe this boss teaches you, by treating you poorly, to have higher self-worth and better emotional boundaries. Human interactions can be so intimate and intense that they are the perfect learning ground. Consider it an "immersion" technique! The angels wanted me to include this form of "relationship" guidance because they said it is quite common.

However, this is no excuse to enter or remain in a toxic relationship. Sometimes we just accidentally bump into or get tangled up with the wrong people and we have to use our free will to get the heck out of Dodge! Other times we were only supposed to be in the relationship long enough to learn the lesson, and we need to make sure we don't overstay this leg of our soul's journey.

But if someone shows up right on time in your life, inspires or causes you to dramatically change or shift, draws you to them, or elicits strong emotions in you (negative or positive), consider that this relationship might actually be Divine guidance.

Action step: *Identify one relationship in your life that feels like a pairing planned by Spirit. Send this person an e-mail telling them everything you think you have learned from them (stick to the positive stuff for diplomacy's sake), and see how they reply or view the relationship.*

10. Angel Whispers

These whispers float up to the surface of your mind when your brain is quiet. This is one reason that whispers can address deeper issues or subconscious blocks: when our minds are still, we have better access to our subconscious, as well as the deeper wisdom of our angels. An image I see to describe angel whispers is fuzzy white dandelion petals floating through the air—you have to be ready and look closely to catch them. This is why angel whispers are so different from angel nudges. Nudges are nagging and persistent. Angel whispers do not urge us to do something, but gently invite us to consider taking action or to ponder something more closely. Like hearing, "Getting sick won't bring her back," in your mind right before you are about to binge and purge.

This could be letting you know that an eating disorder you have struggled with for years is subconsciously tied to your grief over your grandmother's death.

If you are able to receive guidance clairaudiently, an angel whisper will sound fainter or quieter than "normal" clairaudient guidance. (Sometimes my clairaudient voice will get loud in readings if there is something important the angels want me to say, like repeating the word *Frank*, which I later find out is the client's husband's name, or repeating the number nine, which I later find out is the age of one of the client's children). You might hear the word *wait* as an angel whisper softly in your mind right before confronting your boss or your partner about something you want or something you are upset about. Or you might just have the quick flash of a thought that you should wait, or a brief feeling you should wait—also angel whispers. Hearing this means it is probably not the ideal moment to approach your boss or partner about this subject! You might receive a better response tomorrow. This is an example of how angel whispers can be minor course corrections that will make life's journey smoother or more enjoyable. Angel whispers show just how closely the angels follow us throughout the day. They are aware of, and even anticipate, all of our needs and concerns. Nothing about our lives is boring to angels, and they delight in the minutiae of everyday existence.

Action step: *Ask the angels to send you a gentle angel whisper today or tomorrow (better to ask at the beginning of the day to give the angels time to respond). Act on this guidance and note the result!*

11. **Animals and Nature**

This form of angelic guidance will especially resonate with people attracted to Pagan and Native American traditions, as well as folks who are nature and/or animal lovers. Some people feel closest to Spirit or God when they are outside, and often people who are not very spiritual at all will feel a sense of something greater and eternal when they are outdoors. This is because nature is Spirit's church. The angels are giving me an image of a man standing beside a lake in the middle of a picturesque mountain range with his arms held open in awe. This gentleman is experiencing a natural cathedral.

The angels are asking me to relay this warning: "Please take care of these sacred spaces." (At first I accidentally typed "scared" spaces, and the angels told me this is true, especially for the animals in nature who sense that something is "off" or "not right" and changing in a negative way.) When parts of nature are lost or disrespected, humans lose a bit of our connection to Spirit. Look for ways to live more aligned with nature, like reducing your waste and your carbon footprint. Try to eat organic and recycle. Consider donating time or money to a nonprofit dedicated to protecting the earth and animals. This will increase your connection to Spirit and yourself, and actually improve your intuition!

Taking a quiet walk in nature can be a wonderful, quick, and free way to clear your energy. You know those drive-through car washes? The angels have given me a clairvoyant image of the huge sponges that whip over the top of the car as a metaphor for how a walk in nature changes your energy—nature literally *cleans* your energy, just as those enormous sponges clean a car. You can get this effect by walking in any type of nature setting: fields, woods, deserts, mountains, along a beach. If you have a hectic job or work in an open office with a lot of people, taking even a fifteen- or twenty-minute walk in nature will be very restorative! If you are feeling emotionally intense or just had a fight with someone, take a walk in nature to calm down and get your center back. The angels suggest that we make these walks mandatory as a form of maintenance for our energy field and our sanity.

The wind on your face making you feel free after a long day at the office, a storm that suddenly stops you from heading out to run errands so you have time to pick up the call of a friend who really needs a shoulder to cry on, or a beautiful spring day where the flowers seem to rejuvenate your spirits and give you hope about something you are struggling with are all examples of how nature can send us signs.

People will often see images in clouds, especially angels. Sometimes these cloud images of angels will appear over places where a tragedy has just happened. Animals are also wonderful natural messengers, and people often report seeing butterflies or birds as messages from loved ones who have passed on. Pets are often very intuitive.

You might have a "lucky" animal like a frog or an elephant. Then when you go to a new yoga studio, there is only one piece of art on the walls in the lobby or waiting room: a huge photograph of an elephant. Or perhaps you go to interview for a new job, and when you arrive you realize that the frog is part of the company's logo. Seeing your lucky animal can be a good omen about this yoga studio or company.

Action step: *If you have a dream of a giant sea turtle, or start noticing sparrows out of the blue, or keep seeing images of giraffes on t-shirts, mugs, and books, ask your intuition what message this animal is trying to convey.*

ANGEL EXERCISE:
Asking Your Guardian Angels for a Sign

Now that we have covered all eleven magical ways that angels send you guidance, let's ask your guardian angels to communicate with you using one or more of these methods. Angels love to send you guidance that can improve your life, as well as simple reminders of their loving, healing, protective presence, so your guardian angels will be pleased by your request. You can ask your guardian angels to send you a sign either by writing this request in your journal, by offering up a formal prayer, or by asking for a sign in your thoughts. Perhaps you think a few times throughout the day, "I'm so excited for these signs my angels are sending. I'm on the lookout!" Your guardian angels will have no trouble sending you signs. Remember, you have more than one guardian angel on duty, so this is a team effort!

I hear some people saying, "Have my guardian angels been asleep on the job?" Your guardian angels have been supporting you, guiding you, and trying to get your attention your entire life. That is their job, and it's one they do out of love and devotion to you—not because they need a paycheck. Even if you are going through a rough patch or experiencing heartache about something that happened in the past and shook your faith, it's important that you suspend your disbelief while doing this exercise. Entertain the idea, even for a few days or a week, that your guardian angels are very real and always sending you guidance. This attitude will help you receive more guidance, because you will be on the lookout for angelic signs and your more open energy will open up the lines of communication.

One way to increase the amount of guidance you receive at any point in your life is to simply ask for more signs.

Once you ask your guardian angels for a sign, keep your eyes—your physical eyes and your metaphysical third eye—peeled for communications from your guardian angels.

A sign from your guardian angels could take the form of any of the following:

- a prophetic dream
- an unexpected romantic or business opportunity

- hearing a song that holds meaning for you at a significant moment

- being nudged to take action on something you've procrastinated

- a new friend entering your life

- drawing an oracle card with the perfect message for you right now

- getting some sage advice from a friend

- an angel number like 444 appearing often

- an increase in synchronicities (meaningful coincidences)

- your lucky color, number, or animal popping up

- being directed to a helpful book or podcast

- hearing or feeling an enlightening or helpful angel whisper

- nature or an angel changing your mood

- reminders of angels, like finding white feathers on the ground, being recommended movies or books about angels, or seeing images of angels on advertisements or social media

Signs can come from your angels in countless forms. These signs will often be very personal and tailored just to you, because your guardian angels know you so well. If you think something is a sign from your angels, it probably is. The fact that you are actively on the watch for these signs will help you recognize them. When you receive a sign from your guardian angels, you might go to your journal and log it.

You could receive signs for other people. Once I had a friend who was considering going to beauty school, but called to tell me she was on the fence. That same weekend my husband and I were out walking and passed a salon. I had not noticed it, but my husband stopped and glanced in the window. "Wow, it really looked like everyone in there was having so much fun!" he commented as we walked on. "People were smiling and talking and laughing. It looked like a party!" I considered this a good omen for my friend (my husband knew nothing about her dilemma) and called to tell her.

Also, spend some time thinking about the signs you receive this upcoming week. A sign might have meaning on several different levels or contain more than one message for you. The angels are showing me images of Chinese boxes and Russian nesting dolls—things that look like just one item from the outside, but once you examine them, you realize there is always a smaller, similar object inside the outer object. The angels tell me that signs from Spirit are the same. I experience this with clients in readings when I draw oracle cards. As soon as I flip a card over, I will get several messages that this one card wants to give my client about their specific situation.

Here are some straightforward instructions for receiving and interpreting a sign from your angels:
Step One: Ask your angels for a sign in your thoughts, prayers, meditations, or journal. You can ask for a sign about a specific area of your life, like your health or your career. But then give the angels lots of slack about how and when you receive this sign (don't ask to see a white feather on Tuesday afternoon).

Step Two: Go into Sherlock Holmes mode and be ultra-observant. You do not need to stress, but waiting for signs can make you more present in your daily life and help you notice more of the details of your existence—a good thing!

Step Three: When something happens that you think is a sign, test it out with your intuition: Do you get a strong gut instinct that this is a sign from your guardian angels? When you experience this sign, does the energy around you feel denser, slower, or more electric? Does this experience keep popping back into your mind throughout the day or week? Did you get chills or other physical sensations with the sign?

Step Four: Savor the sign, ponder it, and then return to it again a few hours or days later to reflect on and feel into the sign once more, seeing if you can draw out even deeper meanings.

6

INTUITION IS AN ART, NOT AN EXACT SCIENCE: 12 GOLDEN RULES

I ONCE HAD a client ask me, during an Angel Reading session, what the first name of his next wife would be. Since I knew he wasn't even dating anyone, I was about to tell him that I couldn't answer that for him. But before I could respond, I heard this clairaudient message from the angels: "Get out of the house more." This client was putting the cart before the horse. He had not dated anyone in years and wasn't putting himself in situations where he might meet a potential partner: joining a book club, taking a dance or cooking class, volunteering in the community, putting the word out to friends and family that he was interested in finding a romantic partner, or trying online dating. Some folks love being single. This man didn't, but he was expecting his next mate to just fall into his lap. The angels told me that this client had become a real creature of habit. No judgment—we've all been there; we desperately want something to change, but we aren't doing much to make that happen.

Humans get into a routine of work, chores, taking care of animals, kids, ourselves, and other family members . . . and then we get up the next day and do it all again. But when we want something new in our lives, we have to not only carve out some space for it, like making time to attend a weekend workshop where we might meet someone, but we need to break up the routine just to get some fresh new energy flowing into our lives. The angels suggested that even going out into a new spot in nature, like a park the client doesn't normally frequent, would be enough to subtly shift the energy in this man's life and begin attracting a new partner. This is because when we change up our routine and try new things, even tiny ones, we are signaling to the universe that we are ready for change. The angels will usually guide us to the next best action step that will get us closer to our dream. So in regard to finding a wife, the angels' immediate advice for this client was "get out of the house."

Yet this client, by asking me for the name of his next wife, brings up an excellent question: If I am really psychic, why can't I just tell him the name? The answer, unfortunately, is very complex. But we can learn a lot about intuition by examining this question, which we will do in this chapter. The fact that intuition is not an exact science (although really, what is, since our scientific understanding is always evolving) keeps many people from trusting, honoring, honing, or putting any stock at all in intuition. Understanding some of the main guidelines of intuition, outlined in this chapter and the next one, will educate you on intuition and help you better utilize your own intuition. The angels are giving me an image of a sommelier swirling wine around in a glass before smelling and tasting it. I hope that after reading this chapter you will feel like an empowered intuition connoisseur!

When We're Only
Supposed to Know the Next Steps

Intuition Golden Rule #1: *Even when considering major changes in your life, always look for intuitive guidance about immediate next steps. Your intuition will occasionally give you glimpses into the distant future, but by and large your intuition is mainly concerned with the most pressing issues in your life today.*

Why couldn't the angels help me answer the client's question about his future wife's name? Simply put, he hadn't even met the woman yet. Even if he had a strong soul contract where he was destined to meet and marry someone specific, his free will plays a huge role. The angels are reminding me of that old adage that the best things take time. We are meant to move toward even fated events step by step. Occasionally we'll get big-picture flashes, like when lightning strikes on a dark night and allows us a brief glimpse of the horizon, as we will discuss later in this chapter, but we still often make our way to those events inch by inch. It's part of how things work here on earth, which is very different from how they work in the dimension known as heaven.

Imagine sailors hundreds of years ago, on a long ocean journey knowing they are pointing their ship toward Spain. Finally, one morning the sailors see the faint hint of land on the horizon. Now, perhaps they had a fortune-teller on board. How practical would it be for the captain to inquire about what his new life would be like in Barcelona? That is so far in the future. More pertinent is the fact that the maritime psychic senses the boat is entering shark-infested waters. She also picks up on a tiny, as yet undetected leak in the hull. And what about her gut instinct, no pun intended, that the two sailors complaining of sea sickness are really ill as the result of nuts gone bad, fed last night to the whole crew. Perhaps it's best to get all that information from the wise woman on board before worrying too much about what happens once the ship docks. We have to finish getting the ship to Spain in the first place!

Let's say the angels gave me the name Kathy as my client's next bride. Well, what if, heaven forbid, he met a wonderful woman who was not named Kathy? Would he just not date this lovely gal named Susan? She might have been someone he was meant to be in a long-term commitment with before she dies twenty years after they meet. After Susan's death, he may be destined to marry her friend named Kathy, whom he bonded with during their mutual grief. Or what if he meets someone—again, not named Kathy—and really likes them, but the relationship hits the rocks and they break up after a few years. Perhaps this client would learn so much about himself and what he really wants in a partner that he would start to desire the exact attributes Kathy possesses, attributes he'd only appreciate and be attracted to after this "bad" relationship. If he avoids all women except those named Kathy, he will actually never meet Kathy, since it is the relationships in between that lead him to her. The angels are showing me the image of a long novel, and someone flipping through the pages to skip ahead. This client is like a reader trying to read chapter 10 when he has not yet finished chapter 1. If the reader skips that far ahead, he won't even understand what he sees in chapter 10. The angels are reminding me that one thing really does lead to another.

Also, even when we have a soul contract to marry someone, there is still an element of free will choice. So the contract is there in the realm of Spirit, but we may choose not to sign it here on earth. The communication guru, Archangel Gabriel, is telling me that the best way to explain this concept of not being given too much intuitive information too soon is that this life is supposed to be a mystery, to a degree. A thrilling adventure. A once-in-a-*soul*time ride, when we are supposed to learn, grow, experience, and simply feel a full range of emotions.

Just like those sailors, stay present on the journey, moment by moment, so you don't miss those breathtaking ocean sunsets … or those sharks off the starboard bow! The angels will usually guide you to the next best steps for meeting a mate, not give you the name of a woman you may not meet for months or years to come. Or perhaps there are a few possible romantic partners coming up in the future that you will have to pick from, and it's part of your journey to make those decisions on your own.

Sometimes things are simply a matter of divine timing, and before you meet your next partner there are certain growth events and evolutionary processes you need to go through first so you are both "ready" for each other. Maybe you are ready, but they aren't and are still tangled up in another relationship not meant to end quite yet. You might really want to settle down for years, but date many women who never turn into a wife. Then out of the blue you have a spiritual awakening. You start traveling to India, revise your spiritual beliefs drastically, get into meditation, and even adjust your career and life goals based on this awakening. It's probably best to choose your next life partner *after* all those transitions take place, so you can choose someone like-minded. If a client like this, who was going through many spiritual awakenings, asked me for the name of his next wife, I may have told him he would find what he was looking for in India. Not necessarily an Indian wife, I would clarify, but the path that would lead him to a like-minded soul mate would begin with a trip to India.

Spirit and the angels will always give you guidance about what is most pressing in your life today. It might not be finding a mate at all. The angels might be much more eager to encourage you to move homes, re-evaluate your career, make peace with a loved one, give a friend some important advice, or take better care of yourself. Like the sailors on the ocean voyage, these issues might be more immediate concerns on your timeline.

Recognizing the Importance of Free Will When the Future Appears "Fuzzy"

Intuition Golden Rule #2: *Part of what shapes the future are the free will choices you and others make. Because these are free will choices made in the moment, your intuition cannot always predict the future. Your personal free will is your most powerful ally for positively influencing outcomes. Even choosing to have a positive attitude while still expressing your challenging emotions can dramatically affect a situation.*

Utilizing all the tools at your disposal will help you make the most of your human journey and live at your soul's highest potential. One of those tools is your intuition, and another is your free will. The angels say these two assets work hand in hand. When you get an intuitive hit from your angels or higher self, the next step is using your free will to act on that guidance in the best way you are currently able. Sometimes clients will wonder if they think about themselves too much, or should ask more questions about loved ones in a session with me. While I think we each came to this planet with a primary mission of being of service to others, our greatest *power* lies in our ability to change our own lives, to navigate our own futures. That's why understanding that you are a powerful spiritual being with free will is so necessary.

Say a client asks me a question like, "Is this job right for me?" or "Is this city right for me?" or "Is this potential romantic partner right for me?" I usually get a clear answer—meaning yes or no, warm or cold, or often a percentage (angels love to talk to me in percentages) of the odds this option has of working out, since many things are not completely predictable. I can usually get a read on whether there is a strong possibility that this situation can work out well or is something the client should pursue. But occasionally when a client asks me a question about the future of a situation, in reply the angels show me a clear image of a fuzzy TV screen.

People who were adults or kids in the 1980s and 1990s in the US remember that there would be several channels you might not have been able to pick up on your television because they weren't in your cable package. Or you might have just had poor reception and had to adjust the "rabbit ears" on the TV (going way back, here). When you turned to one of these channels, the television screen would be filled with fuzzy, black and white pixels, or what we used to call "static." When the angels show me this static image clairvoyantly, it can tell me something significant: that the "future" is still unwritten, because my client and possibly other people involved in the situation have to make some free will choices around this issue. The angels have shown me that life is like a canvas, and we stand in front of it "gifted" with a paintbrush and a diverse pallet. Our free will is how we co-create our lives. And sometimes the future cannot be seen until we make some free will choices, and then others make free will choices in reaction to ours.

A client who is ill might ask me, "Will I heal?" That type of question may not have a straightforward answer, partly because bodies and healing by nature are not always predictable, and partly because of free will choices. The client might need to pursue several different avenues, doctors, or healing modalities to heal or make a chronic condition manageable, or spend money on things that are not covered by the client's current insurance policy. Being flexible and determined regarding a healing journey falls under the category of free will choice. A client might ask me, "When will I be debt free?" In answer, I might hear two different dates from the angels, years apart. That's because how quickly the client gets their finances in better shape depends somewhat upon free will choices. Maybe the client's partner will prefer to go a little slower with debt repayment so it does not drastically impact the quality of their family's life. Or maybe the client will be guided to a book or healer or workshop that deals with subconscious blocks or negative patterns around finance. Working on this might speed up the process, but the angels can only give the guidance—it will be up to the client to exercise his or her free will and ignore the guidance or act upon it.

"Will my ex-boyfriend ever change?" a client might ask. The angels could give me an image of a much kinder, gentler version of this ex-boyfriend. Instead of verbally abusive, he is encouraging. Instead of controlling, he is supportive. Instead of addicted to alcohol, he is sober. But then I see or hear

"30 percent" in my mind. That means there is a 30 percent chance this man will hit bottom, or see the light. However, there have been people who have pulled off odds of a 1 percent chance! The angels say that these percentages are never meant to discourage you, just to give you an idea of what you are working with in the field of potential. The important thing, the angels say, is that the possibility of someone turning their life around is real! If you love someone and they want to change, do not ever give up on them. But realize that while you can influence their free will choices, ultimately another person's free will is out of your control. You might have to surrender your desire for someone to change, or put healthy boundaries up regarding that person until they do change.

More of this life than we might imagine exists within the boundaries of our free will. The angels say that while you may not always be able to control big stuff—like wars or weather patterns or an illness you get—you can always use your free will to obtain a better quality of life, a better journey.

It's All So Emotional

Intuition Golden Rule #3: *Practice being grounded (doing things to make you feel safe, calm, and confident) to increase intuition. If you are experiencing heightened emotions, like intense fear or anger or just garden-variety anxiety, wait until the emotional storm passes before trying to get answers from your intuition.*

Archangels Gabriel and Uriel are telling me that some-times our emotions can get in the way of or "cloud" our intu-ition. We really want a certain outcome and we think it's for our highest good, so we convince ourselves that our sixth sense is giving us the green light. The angels are telling me now that this is one of the biggest reasons that people will *mistakenly* believe a relationship or situation will work out a certain way based on their own intuitive hunches. "I just feel like it's going to work," they might say. What these people are really *feeling* is their own intense emotions and expectations around this situation.

The angels say intense, heightened emotions can block or distort intuition, which is why you get the clearest, most on-point intuitive hits when you are in a calm, open state of non-attachment. The angels are telling me now that this might be one reason why I'm able to give my clients valuable intuitive advice. While I want the best for anyone who gets a reading with me, I am never as attached to any one outcome for them because it's not my life, so it's *much* easier for me to be objective.

The angels tell me that fear can be another way our emo-tions might block or distort our intuition. Once, right after I got out of college, I was in a bad living situation in a building that was crummy and not very safe. I knew I needed to move and find a better apartment, but looking for an apartment in a big city like mine was intimidating, I had a lot I was coping with at the time, and I hadn't even been in my current place a calendar year. Truly I was terrified at the thought of having to find a new apartment! I kept getting signs that I needed to move. But I ignored those signs, telling myself I was imagining these synchronicities, making up my gut instincts. I actually hear similar stories very often from clients. People will say something like, "Oh, I knew this marriage was doomed from the beginning" or "I had a terrible feeling about my boss from the first time I met her." These clients were all getting clear warning signals from their intuition that they chose to ignore.

In my case with the not-so-ideal apartment, I finally faced my fears, moved, found a dream apartment, and stayed there for many years. Of course the "bad" apartment had its blessings in disguise—it was near a large park so I became very in touch with nature. The "bad" apartment was also near a prominent food co-op, which I joined and remained a member of even after I moved away from the neighborhood. I believe there was a purpose to me being in that apartment. Sure, I could have had higher standards and chosen a better apartment in the same neighborhood from the beginning, but obviously I needed to first learn the lesson that I deserved more. It's the same way my clients experienced blessings in disguise from those "bad" marriages or jobs. These were situations they needed to go through to learn some lessons … and these marriages and jobs were not all bad (they facilitated children, homes, financial abundance, or career experience). It's important to remember that so you don't beat yourself up for ignoring your intuition. Most experiences are brought to you for a reason and have their purpose. If you ignore your intuition telling you something is not right or that you can do better because you are afraid, you might have needed that situation for growth, because you don't yet "trust" that it's not right or that you can do better.

In the past, when I needed to make a big change—like switch doctors or end a romantic relationship—I fought the intuitive hits and synchronicities initially, telling myself they were not real or that they were unimportant, because *emotionally* these changes were overwhelming. A combination of the universe hitting me over the head with guidance and the situation progressively deteriorating finally forced me into action.

It's common for big changes to be accompanied by big emotions. These are occasions when you naturally want to utilize your intuition, but the angels show me that heightened human emotions can create a barrier that makes it hard for intuitive hits to break through. The angels suggest that if you are feeling very emotional about a situation or decision in your life, try to get some healthy coping skills to process your emotions and make them more manageable. This can include leaning on friends and family, talking to a therapist or other health-care professional, journaling, getting lost in a creative project, practicing yoga or meditation, or any combination of these. Once you are feeling calmer emotionally, it will be much easier to touch in with your intuition for clear guidance—and find the courage to follow your instincts.

Are You Picking Up on Something That Will Happen Further off in the Future?

Intuition Golden Rule #4: *Your intuition can give you guidance about something that feels too unlikely due to your current circumstances. Remember that with time, life can change dramatically in very positive ways. If your intuition is encouraging a dream or giving you hope—trust this guidance.*

Our intuition might give us clues about something that will happen way down the line. The problem is that we usually aren't given a date for this event because it is so far away, or the timing of the event is flexible. Therefore, when what we had foreseen does not immediately come to pass, it can make us doubt our original intuitive hit. Also, when we are given information that something will happen in the future, and this will be a drastic change from our current life circumstances, we can again doubt the intuitive hit, thinking, "How in the world can such a large transformation take place?" We are perhaps shown point A and point B, but not the entire path in between.

One day I was at home taking a bath, reading one of Cheryl Richardson's books. A life coach, Cheryl was writing about how she was an author of many books, some of them *New York Times* bestsellers. And then she wrote something like, "And who knows, you could be next!" I remember when I read that line, it felt like she was speaking right to me, even though I was alone with a book that had been printed years before. It was as if I were outside of myself, watching the scene in a movie. I put the book down and stared off into space for a few minutes, pondering the implications.

I had always been a writer and editor and very much wanted to publish a book. I'd gotten close to publishing a novel with a big literary publisher in my late twenties, but the deal went south. And though I had a lot of interest from other publishers, nothing jelled, so I put my book publishing dreams on a shelf. But now, eight years later, Cheryl seemed to be telling me I would write inspirational books—and even be successful at it. Then my logical brain kicked in. "How in the world will I accomplish that feat?" I now realize I was intuitively glimpsing an outcome that was many years in the future.

In sessions with clients, I will often hear the angels say "two years" or "forty-five" about a client, meaning the far-off change is likely to come two years from today or when the client is forty-five. If you get a strong intuitive hunch that something is coming into your life, give the idea a chance. Work toward that goal little by little, day by day. Or perhaps your circumstances will miraculously and dramatically change overnight—as can happen—at some point in the future, in a manner you could never anticipate. We forget that the universe will bring people and opportunities onto our path that we could never foresee at this moment. I had many people and opportunities come into my life that helped me become a published author, though none of them were on my radar that day I was relaxing in the bathtub reading

Cheryl Richardson's book. I also changed a great deal over the next decade, in ways I could have never predicted, ways that lead to the author and intuitive I am today.

So why do we occasionally get these intuitive hits that are from far off in the future? These intuitive hits give us some direction, or a place to point our ship on this soul voyage we call life. These glimpses into the future can also serve as inspiration. Maybe you have been trying to get pregnant for seven long years. At times you consider giving up, but ultimately you don't because you still feel or know in your heart that you will be a mother. This intuitive urging about being a mother keeps you engaged with your dream, and one magnificent day years into the future—whether you adopt, have a child naturally, foster children, or marry someone who already has children—you realize your dream of motherhood.

Not Being Open Shuts Down Intuition

Intuition Golden Rule #5: *You can actually close off or scramble your own or another's intuition if you are not open to guidance or attached to a particular outcome. This can cause a lot of frustration and missed opportunities.*

I would estimate that 99 percent of my sessions with clients are enormously successful. I am able to pull some influential information out of the cosmic ether, and the client walks away feeling impressed, satisfied, inspired, motivated, informed, comforted, or hopeful—or any combination of those. Perhaps that is not so much a testament to my intuition as it is an indication that the angels send me clients that they know I would be a good match for.

However, on a few occasions over many years of giving readings, I have gotten off the phone and felt like the Divine mission the angels sent me on with this client was not a complete success. Certainly I am fallible, and not everything I suggest will resonate, be on target, or feel useful to the client. But people should walk away from a session with enough that they sense a deep gratitude for the angels. On those few occasions when I have sensed that the client is confused or unsatisfied, it's a very frustrating experience. Finding an intuitive you can work with successfully is like any other relationship—it has to be a good fit with some chemistry. Barring a bad fit or lukewarm chemistry, this unfortunate outcome of a client feeling very unfulfilled by a session often is in part caused by not being completely open to the session (this is different than a client being nervous, which is quite natural, and nerves often melt away within the first few minutes of a session).

A client may not be open enough to the session for one of two main reasons: First, they are skeptical about me, my connection to angels, or psychics in general. This can lead the client to be reserved or on guard during the session. The other reason is simply not wanting to hear certain information.

I might start telling the client something they are not ready to hear, or advice they don't believe will be helpful, so they shut down. I always encourage people to run the angelic guidance I receive during a session through their own filters of common sense and intuition. So something I say in a session just may not ring true. But what I'm talking about here are inconvenient truths the client does not want to look at, like maybe it's time to explore new career options or stop enabling a loved one. Or perhaps I suggest the reason the client is not in a relationship is because they are subconsciously wishing to protect their heart by not engaging in romantic affairs. Or suggestions from the angels about how to change or improve their life seem, to the client, like they won't work.

The angels are inviting you to think of the doors to your heart and mind as actual physical doors. When I think of a client who does not trust what I do or does not trust me personally or does not trust what I suggest, I get an image of a gatekeeper in front of those doors who will not let me pass. When I imagine a session where I tell a client something they don't want to hear and they shut down, I get the picture of a steel door slamming closed in my face.

It's so vital to the process to stay open regarding intuition, whether you are relying solely on your intuition or using a trusted intuitive to supplement your own intuitive guidance. As I said before, some psychics will resonate with you while others won't. You might have had a friend who loved a certain product or restaurant or doctor. "You have to try this!" she says. So you go get whatever she is raving about and you do not have anything close to the same experience.

Yet even with an intuitive you don't completely resonate with, there will be some useful messages you receive from the session if you are open. At least initially, give everything they say a chance or some room in your mind, even if you think their suggestion is off base and later decide not to follow the advice. You are always meant to run an intuitive's advice through your own filter of intuition, common sense, and your experiences in the world.

I go into such a state of extreme focus and concentration during a session with a client that it feels like I have stepped out of time and space. My client is in this place with me, as well as their guides and angels and departed loved ones. And for about an hour, or as long as the session lasts, it's almost as if our minds are merged, until the session ends and we go our separate ways. You might be familiar with the Vulcan mind meld technique from *Star Trek*, and whether you are already familiar with it or not, go on YouTube and enjoy some of the campy videos where Mr. Spock places his fingers on someone else's face and uses his telepathy to tune into their thoughts. In actuality, what I am doing, and probably what Spock was supposed to be doing as well, is tuning into someone else's mind, heart, and soul.

The angels are showing me an image of a computer screen and someone trying to hack into a system, randomly and frantically attempting many codes to see which one works. That is what it's like if you are not open to me during a reading. Your system can lock me out. When this happens I can get very anxious or feel on edge. I have learned to recognize this quickly the rare times it ever happens in a session, so that I don't get nervous because something feels "off." Luckily, it has only happened to me a handful of times. I simply recognize that for whatever reason the person is not open to the session. Now that I know this feeling and have a coping mechanism, I have actually had a session I was able to "save." For the first fifteen or twenty minutes the person was very defensive or even combative, but I stayed centered and kept plugging. By the end of the session the client was thanking me and feeling so much happier and more peaceful.

Another possible reason for not being open during a session is the client feeling intensely emotional. Usually if a client is not open in the beginning, they relax and become very open as the session progresses. When I realize a client is not open, I can relax and just do the best I can to deliver them some useful wisdom. I feel like the angels who watch over healers try to do a bit of matchmaking, so the healer's sessions with clients are a win-win for everyone involved.

If you aren't open to your own intuitive hunches, the angels tell me it sends this message to yourself: "I cannot trust my intuition." You may get intuitive guidance from your own higher self that feels out of left field. Maybe a voice tells you you're actually terrified of something you think you desperately want, like buying a new home, going on a long trip, going back to school, starting a family, or leaving a job or relationship. As crazy as it may sound, your intuition is alerting you to subconscious blocks that could be affecting your ability to find a new home or create the time and money to take that trip, and so forth.

Or perhaps your intuition gives you a possible solution to a problem, and your logical mind thinks it will never work in a million years. Maybe you need a loan to start a business, and one night when you are racking your brain trying to think of where the seed money could come from, an image of a distant relative pops into your head. You might contact this person and be surprised to find that the distant relative would be happy to be a bigger part of your life and offer you a loan at a very fair rate of interest. This knowledge about a distant relative who would loan you money is wisdom you could have never come to without your intuition's help. But you need to be open to the guidance to take advantage of it, or there is a danger you will just reject it without even exploring this option.

Remember, your intuition isn't always straightforward. It deals in possibilities and leads you to experiences that facilitate growth. In the example of asking a relative for a loan, your relative may say no. Perhaps they just learned the day before your call that the roof on their house needs major renovations. They don't have any spare money, but they are very supportive and wish they could help. Just the act of calling someone and asking for help, and having that person be kind and understanding, gives you the confidence to do it again. And eventually someone says yes, so you get the seed money you require.

When you are working with an intuitive like me, do your best to stay open to what they say during the session. It does not mean you have to take the intuitive's advice or even agree with it. Be open to your own intuitive hits too, especially the ones that surprise you. They can be the most powerful and useful!

Intuition and the Trickster

Intuition Golden Rule #6: *When you want something that is not for your highest good, the trickster energy of intuition can actually encourage you down a "wrong" or less advantageous path so you can discover that this path was never meant for you or not at all what you hoped. The trickster can also put up roadblocks that force you to slow down and reconsider a situation. Mercury retrograde is an example of this sometimes annoying, yet ultimately benevolent trickster energy at work in the world.*

Sometimes our logical brain will lead us into desiring something, like a career change that really is all wrong for us, and it activates the trickster. This actually happened to me. When I was much younger I spent two years applying to a program that would allow me to go back to school (for free) to be a special education teacher. I wanted something stable, and I wanted to do good in the world. I got a bit of positive intuitive guidance about the career, though looking back, this guidance was rather sparse, not like the flood of guidance I will get when I am truly on track. And every time I had to stand up and teach to kids in a classroom or work with them one-on-one, it was not clicking. In my current career as a psychic, author, and speaker I feel very happy, confident, grounded, fulfilled, and full of energy! While I was trying to become a special education teacher, everything felt off and I felt lost and a little desperate. Yet I even had a psychic tell me that I would be accepted to the program and become a famous special education advocate!

Many things the psychic said in that session about my family and some of my main subconscious blocks were true and helped me greatly. But about my career this psychic was mostly way off … but not entirely. This psychic said I would write many books about these children and rise to some prominence. Well, I did end up writing several books … just not about special education. (Yet many years later I wrote *Zen Teen*, a mindfulness book for teens and preteens.) I now realize the trickster was at work in that psychic session.

My own intuition dropped just enough breadcrumbs for me to keep following that teaching path so I could see where it led: a big dead end sign. It just wasn't for me, which was why I was rejected from the (admittedly very competitive) program two years in a row. At the last minute, after my second rejection, an extra space opened up in the program, and I was contacted to come in and interview for it—but I declined. By then I realized this was not for me, and the second rejection came as a relief. Interesting that the real chance to enter the program arrived after I did enough soul searching to realize this was not my path—all part of divine timing. All our intuitive hits have reason and purpose behind them, and lead us to places we need to go or things we need to experience.

My intuition led me to this program because I had to get far enough along in the process to find out this career was a bad fit for me. Only then could I walk away from that dream forever. I decided to start working on a book, and after that, I began to offer intuitive readings. Archangel Michael says it is important to note that these were heart-centered choices and pursuits. I had no clue if I would find a publisher for that book, and I never suspected I would make a good living as a psychic. I was simply passionate about these things and curious about trying them. Once I was on a path that was my true purpose, the synchronicities and intuitive hits I got about my calling happened more often, were clearer, and much stronger. I also felt calm, safe, and excited about my choices, unlike when I was trying to be a teacher and felt nervous, confused, or desperate. Most important of all, I received many opportunities to write books and give people readings, unlike the special education career where I always felt I was knocking on a door that no one ever answered.

The trickster aspect of our intuition serves a purpose, because sometimes we have to learn things the hard way. We have to fail. We have to be rejected. We have to have a relationship or opportunity explode in our faces before we learn whatever lesson we are meant to learn—maybe simply the lesson that this relationship or career choice or even attitude will never work for us. Seeing something through to its natural conclusion—like forcing on shoes that don't fit and walking around in them all day until you have blisters on your feet—is maybe the best way to learn that something is not right for you.

I have had clients e-mail me months after a reading and say, "You were right! I should not have taken that new job we talked about. But I didn't listen to you and I did it anyway. Now I am again looking to leave my job." Or "You were right! I should have apologized to my sister and made nice. Now the whole family is involved in the drama." These clients listened to their own intuition, not my advice. And that is fine. Your decisions should be primarily made by your own judgment, made up of logical, intuitive, and emotional factors. I, as an intuitive, am merely offering advice. If that advice does not sit well or resonate with you, then do not take it. I can be right and I can also be wrong. You should always trust your own intuition—even when the trickster is running the show. Sometimes it's the only way we really learn and grow. And, as I found out with the psychic who gave me a reading about my career in education, sometimes the trickster even enters a reading.

Potential and Possibility versus Set in Stone

Intuition Golden Rule #7: *Your sixth sense will normally lead you down the most advantageous and probable path. Yet there will always be variables affecting the outcome that no one can predict. Knowing this helps you remain centered if things do not work out as planned, so you can intuitively course correct.*

Many times when predicting the future, angels deal in potential and possibility as opposed to fact. You might have the potential to be a famous singer. Perhaps fame is in the stars for you, and your voice is strong and unique. But do you have the drive or even the desire to sacrifice so much to get to the top? There might be the potential for you and your partner to heal your relationship and have a long marriage. But are both of you committed to getting through the rough patch you're in, making compromises, changing, and seeing a professional couples counselor? Or maybe you do everything "right" to become a famous singer or heal your marriage, and things still don't work out as you plan. There are always X factors in life, and many things are not set in stone. Rest assured that if one thing does not work out, new potential and possibility will show up in your life and be revealed to you. This is the nature of the universe: it's like a garden, and there are continually new shoots emerging. We get as many chances as we need and our path is organic—like us, our destiny is a living, breathing thing. We can never truly be "off" our path, in that case. As with GPS, our life path or destiny keeps course correcting.

You might get the intuitive feeling that there is the potential or possibility for something in your life, but right now that's all it is, a possibility. The angels are showing me a lump of clay. It has the potential to be a stunning vase, although you might decide you don't want a vase. Perhaps you want something simpler and more functional, like a plain bowl.

Or maybe you don't want to learn to throw pottery and you'd rather go outside and kick the ball around with the dog. In many ways, the potential in our lives is dependent upon our free will and the free will of others—and even larger forces in the world, like industry trends and politics and economics. Angels and your intuition will show you potential and possibility. Just because they do not manifest or are not realized does not mean your intuition was wrong.

While I was working on this section of the book, I saw the Kentucky Derby quite by "accident." I was waiting to see a film at a festival and the start time had been pushed back an hour. My friend and I decided to go to a pub down the street and have a glass of wine while we waited. The normally quiet pub was packed and rowdy that evening. I looked up at the television screens behind the bar and realized by the funny hats and serious jockeys that it was Derby Day. Furthermore, the moment we entered the bar, the horses were being walked around for the last time before being put into the stalls at the starting line! We had wandered into the bar ten minutes before the start of a very important yet very short race. The timing was so spectacular I thought it might be Divine timing, that I was brought into that pub at that minute for a reason.

Later I did a little research on the 2017 Kentucky Derby, and found an article from May 7, 2017, on Fortune.com called "Artificial Intelligence Fails on Kentucky Derby Predictions." The article stated: "Unanimous A.I., a company touting the power of collective intelligence to provide insights into the future, correctly predicted the top four finishers of the 2016 Derby." But in 2017, the same system of prediction, which predicted the 2016 winners to an uncanny degree (odds of this prediction were 540 to 1), performed awfully. "This year's top three picks from Unanimous were Classic Empire (actual finish: 4th), McCraken (actual finish: 8th), and Irish War Cry (actual finish: 10th). The Derby's ultimate winner, Always Dreaming, was ranked fourth by the predictive system, with only a 65% chance to finish in the top four," the article reports. (Don't you just love that a horse named "Always Dreaming" was the long-shot winner?) The company behind these predictions had to admit that "some outcomes are just not predictable." That's because in life, as in horse racing, there are always variable factors that are difficult if not impossible to predict: will the track be muddy or dry, will the horse be sick or in top form, what will be the mood of the animal and its jockey, how will all these horses react to each other once they are on the track?

The angels show me an image of an archer and a target. Intuition will give you something to aim for, but it cannot always give you information that guarantees a bull's-eye hit or specific outcome.

Resisting Intuitive Guidance

Intuition Golden Rule #8: *When you find yourself completely closed off to advice or suggestions from others, especially if those suggestions are coming from more than one source, stop and consider that you may be resisting intuitive guidance.*

When my brother and I were growing up in the 80s, we were served meatloaf for dinner about once a month. It wasn't the most glamorous dish, but for a single working mom on a tight budget, it sufficed. Mom and I loved meatloaf, but my brother would always make a face, pick at the food with his fork, and hold us hostage at the table for an eternity waiting for him to finish his "three bite minimum." He would take baby bites holding his nose and then Mom and I would happily eat his leftovers. This went on for years. "Take a real bite and taste it without holding your nose," my mother would suggest. But my brother resisted.

Until one night, much to my shock, he took a bite, chewed, and … smiled. "Hey, this is pretty good!" he announced. "I think I really like meatloaf!" My mother was so upset that she had to leave the room for a few minutes to compose herself!

How many times have you been in my brother's position? Maybe a good friend makes a suggestion about your career, your marriage, your health, or your finances, and you resist it strongly. The friend might dare to make the suggestion again, or perhaps someone else makes the same suggestion, and again you resist it outright without even considering this option. Then years later you find yourself actually doing what your friend suggested, and wishing you had done so much sooner. When one person or several people give you advice and you resist it completely, this may be a sign that what you are actually resisting is intuitive/Divine guidance.

Now sometimes loved ones will give us advice that just doesn't ring true. How do we distinguish *that* advice from resistance to advice that might be intuitive guidance? The angels say one clue is how strongly you resist this advice. If your resistance is absolute, meaning you will not even entertain the advice seriously, or your resistance is aggressive or emotional, these are good signs that you might be resisting intuitive guidance.

Remember, angels love to send you guidance through the people you interact with in your daily life. It's one of the most direct ways for the angels to get your attention!

Perfectionism's Stranglehold

Intuition Golden Rule #9: *Perfectionism treads a very narrow path. Your intuition needs a wide berth to grow strong. Perfectionism deals in right and wrong or black and white, and intuition deals in potential and possibility—as well as interpretation and nuance.*

Perfectionism gets a bad rap. I find that clients with perfectionist tendencies are often very detail-oriented, responsible people who care deeply about the quality of their lives, their work, and their relationships. They are also usually highly sensitive. Extremely sensitive people do not like to make "mistakes" at work, for example, because they can already feel what someone else's emotional reaction will be before a mistake is even made! Childhood wounds from when we didn't feel loved, special, or enough—or someone in our life was very judgmental—can also lead to perfectionism.

When the angels whisper to me during a session that a client has perfectionistic tendencies, I always tell the client that part of being a perfectionist is having very high standards, and there is nothing wrong with that. What is wrong is when we have impossible standards, or we don't know what to prioritize, or we are simply too hard on ourselves, which leads to self-sabotaging perfectionism. This is when perfectionism becomes the opposite of what you intended, and you, along with whatever you are trying to make perfect, actually suffer and are negatively impacted.

As a perfectionist in recovery (it's truly a one-day-at-a-time proposition), I can say from firsthand experience that perfectionism cuts off the air supply to almost every aspect of your life and can be a way to avoid life or create distance (it can also indicate a lack of self-love). The angels have told me that perfectionism certainly cuts off the air supply to our intuition by gripping it with a strangle hold. Perfectionism's hold is so tight that it leaves no room for "error" or, even more important when dealing with intuition, nuance, interpretation, possibility, or growth. In short, your intuition needs room to breathe.

An example: If you started relying on your intuition more and felt it was working to your advantage, and then used your intuition to make a decision and "got it wrong," the perfectionist in you could have a self-sabotage field day. Maybe the decision was to go out on a limb and ask a coworker to lunch, after your intuition told you this person found you attractive. When they turn you down flat by constantly making excuses for why they can't go, you forget all the other times your intuition "got it right," and focus on this one misstep. You are also not leaving room for interpretation and nuances. For example, maybe your intuition knew you needed to toughen up and get used to rejection so you would take more dating risks (trickster energy). Or perhaps your intuition was right and this person *does* like you, but froze up at your invitation—your intuition might have been hoping this situation would bring your coworker out of their shell but it backfired (another person's free will influenced the outcome, which happens a lot in dating).

Perfectionism is ultimately unforgiving. Holding your intuition or someone else's to perfectionist standards is like someone looking at an elaborate tapestry with a magnifying glass. You might find a missed stitch, but what is your reward? *You* have missed out on the big picture and the beauty and inspiration of that work of art. Or think of it this way: Perfectionism is like glass itself. One wrong move and everything shatters. If you engage with your intuition in a perfectionistic way, you will not really be engaging with your intuition, only avoiding it or distancing yourself from it. This is the same way that perfectionism in any area of your life is a delay tactic that keeps you frozen in inaction, trapped spending your energy obsessively worrying about the details, separated from the natural flow, and feeling like you cannot trust life or yourself. If you struggle with perfectionism, don't be ashamed or beat yourself up. It can be one of your greatest spiritual teachers. Ask the angels for help.

When the Trail Goes Cold

Intuition Golden Rule #10: *Feeling into whether something seems warm or cold is a great way to get a quick, straightforward response from your intuition about the potential of a person, place, or opportunity.*

You might have heard psychics talk about something being "warm" or "cold." The angels will also tell me if something is warm or cold during sessions with clients. Warm means it's positive (the relationship, job opportunity, healing modality) and probable. Cold means it's a stretch and maybe not in your best interest. This is similar to when a detective will say the trail has "gone cold," or when someone is getting closer to the truth in a guessing game and their partner will excitedly announce, "You're getting warmer!"

During sessions with clients, this cold sensation is a distant or blank sort of feeling, accompanied by minimal guidance or details coming in. I'm not intrigued and want to move on to something else. When I feel warm about something in the client's life, I get excited, sitting up in my chair. My heart starts beating faster and I want to know more. I might say, "Tell me about this woman you just started dating. I like her!" If something comes in as warm, the angels will want to talk about it, offering us guidance and information and suggesting action steps.

Use this "temperature test," as the angels call it, in your own life. It is not an exact test, just like intuition is not an exact science, but this is a great way to get a general feel for something or someone (you might also feel that something is lukewarm or neutral). If you feel excited and energized about something, that is a very good sign. You will probably start getting regular guidance about this situation from your angels. If you don't feel as attracted to something and you do not receive much guidance, it's almost as if someone turned down the volume on a radio. This means the angels do not want to "encourage" you along a path that is probably "not your own," or not in your flight plan or best interests for this life.

If you get a cold feeling about something, you can always ask your intuition why. Recently a client gave me the names of two towns I had never heard of before, both in different states. "Which one should I move to?" the client asked. I got a very warm feeling about one, but not about the other. When I asked the angels why this town felt cold, they said the client would end up feeling isolated there. When I told the client this, the response was, "That is probably true. There is less of a community in that smaller town and less that I am interested in pursuing there."

Shame and Blocking Intuitive Messages

Intuition Golden Rule #11: *Shame is a toxin that slows down or clogs up your intuition, the same way pipes can get clogged up with unwanted muck and slow the flow of water.*

Shame can be a detrimental yet driving force in our lives. Just as shame can shut down your ability to feel compassion for yourself or affect your desire to improve your life, so can shame "shackle" your intuition. Shame is a toxin that runs rampant in our culture and is much like a cancer cell or a parasite: it goes into your system and wreaks havoc, most notably on your self-image and self-worth. Intuition functions best when you are healthy, as intuition is also linked to your mental, physical, and emotional well-being. The better all your other systems are functioning, the more your intuition will have a solid foundation upon which to operate and grow. And shame weakens many of our systems.

Intuition sends us messages to be kinder, softer, and less judgmental toward ourselves and others. But shame blocks out intuition, which can lead to lack of self-love. How we treat others is a reflection of how we treat ourselves. If you are unforgiving with others, you are probably unforgiving with yourself. If you are curt or short with others, you probably are not able to spend much time on you either. If you find yourself being judgmental of others and want to break this pattern, start with being less judgmental of yourself. Among other possible benefits, it will significantly improve your intuition!

Shame can make the world seem like a very dark place, and your intuition thrives on optimism. Shame makes the world look like a place where we make a mistake and then are punished for it eternally, shut out of Spirit's mercy and grace. These shame beliefs can be buried very far down in our subconscious where they were planted by our families decades ago or crept in through cultural programming. The problem with these buried self-sabotaging beliefs is actually twofold. First, your subconscious is the soil from which many things grow. Second, when something is hidden in our subconscious it's harder to discover and bring out into the light. The good news is that we can heal that shame.

Archangel Michael would like to help you do a shame detox. Archangel Michael is encouraging you to do the following exercise even if you don't feel like you are carrying around any shame toxins. He tells me that because shame is emphasized so much culturally, you can catch the toxin that way, just like you can catch the common cold.

ANGEL EXERCISE:
Shame Clearing and Release with Archangel Michael

This will be an energy-clearing exercise, so go to a quiet room where you can shut the door and be alone for fifteen or twenty minutes. Sit in a comfortable position and spend a moment breathing in and out. Archangel Michael is already with you, helping you get grounded as he tunes in to your energy.

1. Ask this question aloud or silently: "Archangel Michael, what event or relationship, from the past or the present, has me carrying around the most shame?" Now close your eyes and see what answers come. You might see someone's face, or hear a name in your mind, or see an image of yourself doing something in the past or present, as if you are watching a movie in your head. You may just get a strong intuitive knowing

about what is causing you the most underlying shame. Archangel Michael says that doing this portion of the exercise is key, because sometimes our shame and its source can be hidden in the subconscious, which our intuition can help us tap into.

2. Now that you have a clear image of your biggest source of shame, we can begin to heal it. Archangel Michael is telling me how healing it can be to practice forgiveness in regards to shame issues. Since Spirit and the angels forgave you instantly, no matter how dramatically you betrayed yourself or someone else, you need to work on forgiving yourself. State aloud or silently: "Archangel Michael, please help me forgive myself and lay down the burden of this shame."

3. Archangel Michael now wants you to think of all the pain this incident and the shame have caused you. Then he wants you to wrap your arms around yourself and give yourself a long hug. Archangel Michael's loving energy will also be encircling you. If tears come, don't fight them. Archangel Michael has a way of bringing to the surface very strong emotions in us, so have a cleansing cry.

4. Archangel Michael says that sometimes we can be hard on ourselves because someone was hard on us and unforgiving toward us when we were children—a parent, a teacher, a sibling. Archangel Michael says that someone who was hard on you during your childhood should

immediately come to mind. Just know that this person's misguided treatment of you is part of the reason you are feeling shame and being hard on yourself today. Now, Archangel Michael wants you to tune into who is your harshest critic in the present. Is it you? Your boss? Your child or spouse?

5. Archangel Michael wants to do a simple energy-clearing exercise to help you get rid of this shame toxin. Like an inoculation, it will have a potent, immediate effect. But you need to follow up this energy clearing with being less judgmental of yourself and others, and being kinder and gentler with yourself to keep feelings of shame about this or any other issue to a minimum. First, close your eyes (read ahead before you do) and imagine Archangel Michael beside you. He is a big, tough, warrior angel with a heart of gold. At his side is a sword of light. He uses it now to cut any cords you have to this memory and to your shame. He does this by passing his sword of light around your aura, or the energy field that surrounds your physical body. You can picture this aura, the angels tell me, as soft, rainbow colors. Imagine Archangel Michael passing his sword of light around your aura for a minute or so until you experience a feeling of lightness. Then Archangel Michael will put each of his hands on either side of you, a few inches from your body. Healing light that is pale blue, a color of mercy, emanates from

his hands. Sit for a minute or two as he continues the healing. Now open your eyes and thank Archangel Michael.

6. Archangel Michael suggests that this upcoming week you now find someone you can forgive. It could be a neighbor whose dog poops on your yard or an old co-worker who threw you under the bus years ago. Only offer forgiveness if it feels authentic to you. Some-times forgiving others gets us in the habit of forgiving ourselves.

7. Archangel Michael says you can picture the shame you have around this issue as a huge, heavy brick you carry around in a backpack all the time. Archangel Michael wants you to imagine that backpack is empty now, and instead of bricks, it is filled with heart-shaped balloons that are weightless. Archangel Michael tells me that letting go of shame can have a "profound" effect on your life and improve your circumstances and rela-tionships. Shame makes us want to punish ourselves, sabotage ourselves, or withhold love and joy from ourselves, when we all deserve the best!

8. Repeat this exercise in a week or so if shame is a major issue for you, shame was emphasized in your house as a child, or if you sense that shame has been holding you back. You can perform this exercise any time you feel the shame toxin creeping into your energy field!

When a Psychic or Your Own
Intuition Simply Gets It Wrong

Intuition Golden Rule #12: *Always leave room for a margin of error with intuition, and remember that no one bats a thousand.*

The phrase "batting a thousand" means being successful on every attempt. This will not be true with your intuition or anyone else's. It's the same way that one of your favorite filmmakers might put out a movie that really isn't so great, or your favorite barista will one day make you a latte that you just can't even finish.

I've given you a few examples in this book of times when I went to a psychic and some part of their prediction for me was just way off. This also happens to my clients. I might ask a first-time client if they are in finance and turns out they not only do *not* work in finance, but they are terrible with money and numbers. Or I might sense they have two children … when the client is in their sixties and never had any children! I used to be terrified of this happening when I first began giving readings, and now I almost welcome it, because it keeps me humble. We can talk about trickster energy, or say that perhaps I was picking up on nieces and nephews or pets who are like children, but I think it's much more powerful to just admit that sometimes your intuition will just plain old get it wrong.

People tend to discount psychics altogether or put them on a pedestal. Neither stance is true or helpful. I'm not all-knowing. I'm simply a human with above-average intuition, sharpening that talent every day with clients and doing my best to be of service. So take intuitive advice from someone else or yourself with the proverbial grain of salt.

The wonderful byproduct of having your intuition be off base about something is that it teaches you humility. I like people to have a healthy sense of confidence in their own worth, but I have to admit that the folks I'm most attracted to—as healers or friends—are the people who can admit that they are what one of my favorite spiritual teachers calls "flawsome." (That's a hybrid between the words *flawed* and *awesome* ... the perfect way to describe humans, right?) I heard a well-known and respected intuitive say that if she got something wrong in a reading, that could still be useful to the client. It could trigger the client's *own* intuition to say, "Actually, that's not right. I know in my heart the truth is something else." In that way this intuitive was still being useful to their clients even when she got something in the reading wrong.

I once had a friend who, when she first started seeing a psychic, followed the psychic's advice to the letter. It was as if she believed the psychic had all the answers. Unfortunately, no one has all the answers. The most you can hope for are pieces of the puzzle.

After reading this book, paying more attention to your intuition, and flexing your intuitive muscle, you will get more—and more accurate—intuitive hits. But occasionally you will still get things wrong. Accept it as part of life and part of being human.

7

HONING YOUR INTUITIVE CHOPS: 13 MORE GOLDEN RULES

In this chapter, I asked the angels to give me some clear guidance on how we can all improve our intuition. Some of the information below I have been preaching for a long time, although some of it came as a surprise—information given to me straight from the Divine. That is the amazing thing about improving and utilizing your intuition—your spiritual guidance squad often gives you insight that you would have never come up with on your own. It's partly why I so enjoy being an intuitive—it's always enlightening to hear the advice that angels have to offer my clients!

Divine Guidance Is a Two-Way Street

Intuition Golden Rule #13: *The more energy you put into asking for, interpreting, and thanking Spirit for signs and guidance, the more signs and guidance you will receive.*

"How can I improve my intuition and receive more Divine guidance?" This is a question I'm asked regularly by clients. Your relationships with your intuition and your angels are like any other relationships in your life—the more you put in, the more you get back. Yet honing your intuition or receiving more Divine guidance should not feel like hard work. It should feel fascinating and fun! Certainly reading books like this one helps, but really what is mainly required is that you remain "present" every day.

Remaining present means watching for clues from the universe, and the more you are attuned to angelic guidance, the more you will receive and recognize it. This is a very subtle way to interact with the angels and receive more guidance, because it's basically a shift in your energy or attitude. But angels are acutely sensitive beings and will pick up on this subtle shift and know that you are now looking for more clues from them. The angels are showing me an image of a scavenger hunt, with children racing around, trying to find the clues, searching under leaves or behind hedges. The angels say that just like parents delight in hiding these treasures and watching children discover them, so do angels love to place more Divine guidance clues in your environment once they know that you are out there on the hunt. This state of mind will also make you more "discerning," as far as what is and what is not Divine guidance. In time, you will spot it more quickly and understand the guidance more fully.

Another way to interact with Spirit and your angels to increase Divine guidance is to enter into a formal agreement with your angels regarding this matter. You can write your angels a journal entry, telling them that you are feeling lost in general, or that you need some specific guidance about your health or love life or whatever is your top priority. Or you might say a quick prayer or meditation each morning, letting your angels know you'd love some guidance during the day and that you will be on the lookout for it. There is no one magic formula to use for increasing guidance. Instead, the angels explain that the more "intentional" you get about asking for guidance, the better.

The intentionality comes from communicating to the angels that you want more guidance, and then doing things like thanking them for that guidance when it arrives, acting on it, and recording signs you receive in a journal. When you ask for guidance from angels you receive guidance. It's that simple, the angels say. Cause and effect.

Making Space for Your Intuition and Creating Sacred Time

Intuition Golden Rule #14: *Quiet time alone calms your nervous system, which helps you open up to more intuitive guidance. When you make space in your life, your intuition will expand.*

The angels told me that one of the best pieces of advice they can offer about how to improve your intuition and receive more Divine guidance is to simply make room for it. I have heard this same advice from the angels in sessions with clients who are looking for a romantic partner, business opportunities, or creative inspiration. The first thing we need to do to make room for more of something in our lives, on an energetic level, is to create some open or "free" time, which signals to the universe that we are ready to receive.

When people think of working on or exploring their spirituality, for instance, their heads might become filled with images of Buddhist monks chanting for hours every day, or Elizabeth Gilbert, author of *Eat, Pray, Love*, taking several months of her life off to travel around the world so she could have the experiences to write a mind, body, spirit bestseller. Maybe to improve your intuition you believe you need to enroll in a mystic boot camp or adhere to an all-vegan diet. The angels want to assure you that making drastic changes to your daily life is not necessary to explore your spirituality or improve your intuition. However, you *do* need to make room in your life for you and your intuition to expand.

Modern life puts so many demands on our time, and culturally we are encouraged to go, go, go! Accomplish more, do more, be more. Many clients tell me their days are so full of work, family, and to-do lists that there is little chance to spend precious alone time reading, reflecting, or communing with nature. Occasionally, I will ask a client who is a working mother if she is able to get a little time to herself each day, and the client will simply laugh in response! Yet intuition blossoms with alone time. The angels are showing me an image of a plant growing very fast, like in time-lapse photography. Quiet moments on your own, preferably hours every week or even just a half hour every day, are like the perfect soil, water, and sunlight for your intuition.

Now, I'm not suggesting you become a hermit! As I have said many times in this book, angels love to send us guidance via the people in our lives, so you need to be interacting with friends, family, coworkers, and even strangers in the grocery line to fully utilize your intuition. But carving out a little time every day, and certainly some time every week, when you are doing something alone and meditative—like exercising, reading, journaling, working on a creative hobby, sitting in nature, or spending time with animals—is essential for improving your intuition. And there is no shortcut for this step. In the stillness and the quiet is when intuition can speak the clearest.

During one of the busiest times of my life, I created a practice called Sacred Saturdays. I realized for optimal self-care I needed a day off (more or less), so I chose Saturdays. I made a few rules for my Sacred Saturdays: I could not do any "work," even if it was work I loved. (Sometimes book deadlines or last-minute readings with clients meant that only half or a majority of the Saturday was work free.) I had to do other things that my soul craved besides work, and I had to spend some portion of that day alone. My husband and I are very close, but I quickly got in the habit of spending an hour and a half on Saturday afternoons at a great coffee shop across the street from my apartment. I'd order a decaf non-dairy latte and avocado toast and read a novel. Living on the edge! I joke about the wild life after forty, but you need to make some sacred alone time for yourself whatever your age.

It might be working out alone a couple times a week, meditating at your altar for twenty minutes before work every day, giving yourself an oracle card reading on a Sunday afternoon, listening to a podcast while taking a bubble bath with the bathroom door closed, taking the dog for a long walk, gardening alone every Saturday, or even just giving the house a good cleaning when everyone else is gone and you can jam your favorite tunes. If you make a point of spending some time alone with no distractions on a regular basis, your intuition will thank you for it.

Intuition and Rituals

Intuition Golden Rule #15: *Tools and rituals can help you focus your intuition, but they are ultimately unnecessary since your intuition is ever-present.*

"What do you have to do to prepare for a psychic reading?" people often ask me. I get the impression they think I have to clear my chakras, light a candle, say a prayer, or perhaps raise my hands to the sky as my wizard sleeves trail on the ground. The short answer is: I don't *have* to do anything special or ritualistic to tap into my intuition, and neither do you. I don't even have to do anything to "summon the angels." The angels are always right there for me, ready, willing, and able … just as angels are always right there for you.

However, there are a few rituals that I find helpful with my Angel Readings. I like to have nature sounds on before I do a reading—this helps calm and relax my nervous system, and when we are feeling calm and relaxed it is easier to tap into our intuition. And while I am talking to the client, I usually hold a set of prayer beads I bought for four dollars from a Buddhist monk at a benefit in New York City. (There's proof that "tools" do not have to be expensive!) I find that holding these beads or some amber or a crystal or another type of stone is very grounding and connecting. I first heard of this practice over a decade ago when listening to the late Dr. Wayne Dyer's radio show. "I cannot decide if I should sell my house and move across the country for this job or not," a caller said. Wayne replied, "Hold on one moment—I just want to grab something before I answer. There's a little stone I like to hold sometimes when I'm connecting to my intuition. It helps me focus."

I also spritz the room with some essential oil aromatherapy spray before I get on the phone with a client, which is a quick and easy way to clear the energy of a space. It helps to put some positive thoughts into the air as you spritz, like imagining the room filled with angels or peace or love. Sometimes I like to have fresh flowers in the room—which raises the vibration of any room! Flowers really help if you are having a day when you feel a little tired or blah.

The main benefit of these small rituals is that they focus the mind. So these rituals remind me that I'm about to go into a sacred space of deep concentration and connection with a client. It's the same way some people like to light incense or strike a singing bowl before entering meditation.

Yet most of your intuitive insights will not happen when you sit down, concentrate, and channel information for an hour straight, as I do in an intuitive reading. Usually intuitive hits happen on the fly—when you are at work, talking to a loved one, cleaning the kitchen. If you want to begin a regular meditation practice where you check in with your intuition in a structured way daily or weekly, you can always strike a singing bowl or burn incense to get yourself in the mood or put on soothing music to calm your nervous system. But know that the only thing you absolutely need in order to access your intuition or your spiritual guidance squad is you.

Opening Wide

Intuition Golden Rule #16: *Meditation helps quiet the mind. When the mind is quiet, your intuition can be heard more clearly and speak more often, because you are more open. Staying open to all your intuitive hits will increase guidance.*

In *Catching the Big Fish: Meditation, Consciousness, and Creativity*, filmmaker David Lynch likens coming up with creative ideas to fishing. You have to go way down into the deep waters of the mind or collective unconscious, Lynch explains, to find the brilliant ideas, or the "big fish." The same metaphor can be used on intuition. And we get into those deep waters of our intuition by remaining wide open.

David Lynch is a huge proponent of meditation, and has even started a foundation dedicated to "healing traumatic stress and raising performance in at-risk populations." The foundation works with kids, veterans, the homeless, prisoners, patients, and more. But really, anyone can benefit from meditation, and the angels often recommend it to clients. It teaches you to quiet the mind, and when the mind is quiet, you are much more open to intuitive guidance.

Meditation Tips:

1. In his book *Getting in the Gap*, Dr. Wayne Dyer describes meditating as increasing the space between thoughts. Play with creating more silence in your mind by seeing how many moments of quiet you can create in between your thoughts. Work on increasing that gap. The gap is where the really good stuff is!

2. Sometimes it is easier to make the mind relax if the body is active, one of the principles behind yoga. Gentle exercise like walking or repetitive tasks like cleaning or grocery shopping can be perfect times to practice meditation.

3. Stimulants like sugar and caffeine will, for many people, jack up the nervous system and make it harder to quiet the mind. The calmer you are, the easier it will be to meditate. But the reverse is also true: even attempting to meditate can help you cultivate more calm.

4. Our brains can be very active when we first wake up and right before bed as our minds begin planning or reviewing the day, which makes these perfect times

to spend ten or fifteen minutes in silent meditation. This will set the tone for the day or help you get a better night's sleep.

5. I have been told by the angels in sessions with clients that people who are naturally high-strung or have very active minds can become physically exhausted just from racing thoughts. Calming the mind can increase physical energy.

6. Often the brain will try to review the same thoughts over and over or create imaginary fights or confrontations with people. Think of these as little fish you choose to let swim by and don't engage with.

7. Fighting or arguing with our unwelcome thoughts will only increase them. If your brain is being overactive, try not to get frustrated or start beating yourself up. Distract or redirect your mind with a mantra, gratitude, or thoughts of self-love. Sometimes if you want the mind to let go of something, you have to give the mind something else to grab onto.

Another way to stay open is to not judge or immediately reject an intuitive hit. If you get a gut instinct about something or an aha idea pops into your head out of the blue, try not to attach any thoughts or emotions to it. Attempt to sit with intuitive guidance and give it a chance. Lynch believes artists have to honor their creative ideas and take the fish (or creative idea they "catch" from the ether) to market. You may not always follow your intuitive hits, or you might even find that some are better than others. But give all of them the attention they deserve.

If you ignore one big message from your intuition continually—like a message to be kinder to yourself—it will drain your intuition's power, much like a battery is drained. Your intuition is holistic in this sense. You cannot accept or embrace only some of its messages unless you want to negatively affect its overall performance. You may not want to get guidance that you should quit your job, find a new partner, start a family, or move back home. But if you block these big or inconvenient messages from your intuition, the smaller or more welcome ones will be harder to hear as well.

After you give intuitive guidance a chance to "sink in," get your mind and emotions involved. The best decisions are made when all three—the mind, emotions, and intuition—are allowed a seat at the "negotiating" table. Be wide open to input from all of them!

Practicing Exceptional Self-Care

Intuition Golden Rule #17: *Basic self-care may sound pedantic, but earthy and foundational practices like eating well and getting enough rest are some of the best ways to increase or tune into your mystical abilities.*

In *Angel Insights*, I discussed my "Third-Eye Diet," which basically means minimizing toxins, eating clean, and living more aligned with nature. This includes avoiding or mini-mizing caffeine, sugar, and alcohol. Organic produce and ani-mal products from animals that have been treated humanely are key. It's also very common that people have certain food sensitivities these days, so getting your doctor to run a blood test or going on an elimination diet to determine if you or anyone in your family has certain food allergies might be important. Get rest, engage in moderate exercise, and take your supplements!

I personally think it's crucial to partner with a health-care professional to make sure you are receiving all the vita-mins, minerals, and other nutrients your adrenals, thyroid, nervous system, gut, brain, and everything else need. Taking these steps to clean up your diet and improve your health will go a long way to improving your intuition. My clairaudi-ence, or the ability to hear intuitive guidance as a voice in my head, came online in my late twenties when I cut out alcohol, sugar, and caffeine and switched to an organic and generally much healthier diet. I took these measures for health rea-sons, and significantly increasing or discovering my intuitive abilities was an unexpected bonus. However, always discuss any major changes to your diet or additional natural supple-ments with a health-care professional.

Now that I am much physically healthier, I do enjoy a glass of wine or two now and again, and I always have a bag of dark chocolate-covered almonds in the fridge! (I also have a weakness for potato chips, but I can blame that on my Irish roots, right?) So by no means am I suggesting you live "like a monk," although I'm sure modern monks are probably fans of chocolate-covered almonds too. What is required is not being perfectionistic with your diet (remember how perfectionism cuts off the oxygen supply to your intuition), but simply being more mindful of what you put in your mouth and how your food choices affect the environment.

The angels suggest eating "clean" for three weeks (cutting out or back on alcohol, sugar, caffeine, high-glycemic carbs and fruits, and anything you think you have a sensitivity to, like dairy, while emphasizing organic food, protein, filtered water, healthy carbs, and veggies) and then seeing how your intuition responds. Are you more sensitive to energy? Are your gut instincts easier to tune into? You might be surprised and delighted by the delicious results!

Processing Your Emotions and Remaining in Your Own Emotional Skin

Intuition Golden Rule #18: *Your emotional health has a direct effect on the health of your intuition and your level of intuitive ability.*

It's common for people to avoid or even block out challenging emotions like fear, anger, or grief. But when you start to block out those messier experiences, you begin to block or dull *all* your emotional responses, and this hinders your intuition. The majority of people do not experience clairvoyant visions or clairaudient voices on a regular basis (although you may have more potential in this area than you realize and just because you have not experienced these things yet does not mean you won't in the future). However, clairsentience is the most common of the intuitive gifts, and the majority of my clients are either very strong in clairsentience or have the capacity to be so (and possibly the capacity to experience more of the other clairs on a regular basis as well).

Clairsentience is all about feelings—both the dramatic, intense feelings and the subtle shifts in energy of people or places. Your intuition can communicate guidance to you through feelings, like giving you the feeling that it's time to end a job, a relationship, or simply a night out on the town. You might be house hunting and get the feeling your realtor isn't the best fit for you, or that the first house you tour is perfect for you. Challenging feelings like fear can tell us when we are pushing ourselves too far too fast, or they can let us know that we're in the middle of a thrilling adventure. Intense grief lets us know how much someone meant to us and that we might have a space in our life that we now need to fill with something or someone new. Anger might let us know where our boundaries are and that someone has crossed them.

Being open to the full range of human emotions greatly increases your sensitivity, which will make it easier for you to pick up on even the most refined, subtle clairsentient guidance from your angels and your higher self. I believe the higher self loves to send you intuitive information through clairsentience.

If you're having difficulty working through complex feelings or want to go back and process old emotions from past wounds or traumas, don't be afraid to ask for help and support from trusted loved ones and health-care professionals—as well as angels. In modern spirituality there is an emphasis on the "lesson" when something bad happens (financial loss, divorce, death of a loved one, health issues, friendships that end). Some people concentrate very hard on the lesson from this experience as a way to minimize or block out any challenging emotions connected to the event.

Another way to increase your clairsentience is by remaining in your own emotional skin. How can you be alert to all the clairsentient information your intuition sends if you are codependent, tracking someone else's emotions, merging emotionally with a coworker or client who is in pain or struggling, or constantly anticipating the emotions of people at home or work? It's especially important for sensitive people to be vigilant about their emotional boundaries, as very sensitive people are so easily drawn into another's emotional field. With practice you will quickly be able to realize when you are no longer centered in your own emotions and then course correct.

Often when people are sensitive and they pick up on the emotions of another individual or even a crowd, the sensitive person feels this emotion as if it were their own. The angels say this is how the emotion registers. So if a friend is feeling chaotic and ungrounded, the sensitive person will actually feel that way too, briefly. The angels say it's important to let that emotional information about the people around us register, but then we must tune out again. This requires practice and a degree of emotional mindfulness. But it's truly possible. If I get on the phone and sense a client is feeling very scared, nervous, or down, this emotional information will hit me strongly. But then I make the conscious choice to simply note the intuitive information and then come back to my own emotions. It really is as simple as a conscious choice. Sensitive people are not at all at the mercy of other people's energy and emotions.

Of course, there will be times when loved ones or coworkers are so stressed or sad that it will be difficult to tune out entirely. Just being aware that it's harder for you to tune out during these times of crisis will help immeasurably. Getting enough alone time, practicing great self-care, and being aware of when you are tuning in to someone or when someone else's energy is affecting you really helps sensitive folks come back to center and live in their own emotional skin.

And don't forget that some people have a strong or almost overpowering energy signature. Occasionally I have clients say that it's difficult to tune out the energy of an overbearing manager or a relative who lives with them. Also, if you have a coworker or relative that is often angry or frazzled, this type of energy contains a strong signature (you can liken it to a pungent cheese). Just being aware that you are dealing with a strong energy will help you cope.

Having healthy emotional boundaries can help us get more clairsentient guidance from our intuition. Otherwise our emotional and intuitive radar can be jammed by the frequencies of others.

Tips for Staying Grounded

Intuition Golden Rule #19: *The best launching pad for your intuition to take off from and soar is a grounded self. When you are grounded you are less likely to get confused about intuitive guidance or misinterpret fear or wishful thinking as intuitive guidance.*

As a psychic, it's important that I remain grounded to give my clients the best my intuition has to offer. When people are grounded they generally feel safe, confident, hopeful, and calm. Times of transition, uncertainty, major losses, or crisis can all be triggers that make us feel ungrounded. Likewise, times when you are experiencing big wins, such as receiving a financial windfall, falling in love, getting the dream job, or starting a family can also lead to feeling ungrounded. Being incredibly busy, with no time to pause and reflect, is also destabilizing or ungrounding.

How does being ungrounded hinder your intuitive abilities? When I ask the angels for an image of what it is like when a human becomes ungrounded, I get a picture of the earth knocked off its axis. We might think of the soul as a human's axis. Since much of our intuitive information comes from our higher self (or soul) and entities, like angels, who have a direct connection to our soul, when we are ungrounded or knocked off our axis, we do not have ideal *access* to our soul or our intuition. Basically, when we are ungrounded we are not connected to ourselves, and if we are not connected to ourselves, how can we be connected to our intuition?

I would like to share advice on staying grounded that has been given to me specifically by the angels.

Picture a happy outcome. Imagining a positive resolution when you are experiencing a challenge is half the battle, the angels have told me. Visualizing a positive outcome will stop you from hand-wringing over worst-case scenarios, which can make you feel ungrounded. And visualizing things working out will actually have a healthy effect on your behavior and the energy you send out to others and the universe. You don't need to get specific with these images or know how the happy outcome will happen or when. If people in your family are fighting, for example, simply picture them getting along—sitting down to dinner together, laughing, or hugging each other hello. The act of picturing a happy outcome will also calm you emotionally and physically, making you feel more grounded.

Stay flexible. Often during crisis people have a tendency to shut down and close up. This is a primal reaction meant to protect you, but it actually does the opposite. While you want to stay secure during crisis or transition, it's imperative that you also remain flexible so that you are open to all the options, possible solutions, offers of help from loved ones, and guidance from the universe. When we are grounded we feel safe, which naturally makes us more flexible. So fake it til you make it—just keep telling yourself to remain flexible and you will trick your mind and heart into feeling safe and grounded.

Use the healing power of touch. When we don't feel grounded, part of the problem is that we don't feel grounded on this physical earth dimension, almost as if we don't feel grounded in our own bodies. The angels have told me that touch is a wonderful way to bring us "back down to earth." If you have a cuddly pet, put them on your lap while you're working on the computer. If you have a child or are living with a romantic partner, hold hands when you walk to the store or snuggle up on the couch while you're watching a movie. If you are living alone, get a massage or make a point of giving friends a big hug hello and goodbye when you get together.

Avoid stimulants and depressants. When we feel ungrounded, having a double latte or an extra glass of wine with dinner is like throwing gasoline on a fire. If you're feeling ungrounded and shaky, throw your adrenals and your nervous system a life preserver by avoiding excess caffeine, alcohol, and sugar. Caffeine is especially hard on sensitive people, and I have been guided to tell a few clients that even green tea is too much for their systems.

Listen to nature sounds. We've all experienced how calming soft, gentle music can be, but it's particularly important to listen to nature sounds. That's because nature is so grounding that often a mild bout of anxiety can be alleviated by a walk in the woods or along the beach. But many of us live in places with intense seasonal changes and spend part of the year indoors. Or perhaps you're in a big city where it's hard to get regular contact with nature. Listening to nature sounds can be especially helpful at night just before bed or if you're having trouble calming down after a hectic day or a fight with a loved one.

Make contact with Spirit daily. Developing a daily spiritual practice, whether it's meditating for fifteen minutes every morning, journaling to your angels each night, or spending more quiet moments in nature, can make a hard time or a transition time a lot easier to bear. That's because Spirit is so grounding. Reminding yourself of what is bigger than you, and the eternal nature of your soul, will help you put yourself and your current problems in better perspective. Being able to put things into perspective is the sign of someone who is currently feeling grounded. I say currently, because we will all have times when we feel temporarily ungrounded!

Find the rhythm to your days. Routine makes humans feel incredibly comforted. Too much predictability can be boring or stifling, but when you are feeling ungrounded, finding a routine that works for you is very stabilizing to your emotions and nervous system. It can be as simple as waking and going to bed at the same time every day, attending the same yoga class once or twice a week, getting your morning tea or coffee from the same shop, reading a favorite book every day on your lunch break, taking a walk on a favorite nature trail every day after work, reading a series of novels about the same characters or reading several nonfiction books by the same author, or having a phone date with a loved one at the same time every day or week. If you are going through a lot of changes and feeling ungrounded, adopt a few regular—pleasurable and healthy—activities.

Indulge in healthy escapes. Crafting, writing, sports, photography, cooking, gardening, woodworking, running, biking, painting, pottery, jewelry-making, researching your ancestry—if you are feeling ungrounded, pick a hobby and dive in! It will keep your mind from racing and worrying, and give you a chance to blow off steam with something fun. Even getting lost in a great miniseries or giant puzzle, the angels tell me, can fit the bill. The angels often recommend that clients take classes or workshops, which is a great way to meet people, get exposed to new ideas, and be more *interactive* with life, which is always grounding.

Trusting Yourself, Trusting Your Intuition

Intuition Golden Rule #20: *Trusting your intuition takes practice, and starting small helps. If you have been through something traumatic recently, you might find it more difficult to trust yourself and your intuition for a while. Be gentle with yourself and remember that you are always connected to your wise higher self!*

Trusting ourselves is not always easy. Often I will get clients who have been divorced or gone through a traumatic breakup and have trouble dating or committing afterward. The angels usually tell me that it's not that the client doesn't trust their new romantic partner or that they distrust love or potential romantic partners in general. Interestingly enough, the person the client does not trust is themselves. They might feel that they made a poor choice in their mate last time around or that they made poor choices in the relationship. They are usually aware on some level that their fears about dating or commitment are tied to past romantic wounds. Of course they *can* trust themselves, because they have learned and grown from those old wounds and will make wiser choices going forward. The more you trust yourself, the more you will naturally trust your intuitive instincts.

Be vulnerable enough to give your intuition a chance. Start with something small, so that even if you follow your intuitive guidance and it leads you to a place you don't like— it's still no big deal. Here is a quick exercise in trusting your intuitive guidance:

Step 1. Flip back to the table of contents of this book and look through the exercise list.

Step 2. Ask your intuition silently, "What exercise would be most beneficial for me to concentrate on now?"

Step 3. Wait for an answer. You might hear one of the exercise titles spoken into your mind (clairaudience) or you might scan the sections and get a strong energy or feeling off of one of the section titles (clairsentience).

Step 4. You can also try this: Ask your intuition for a number between one and fourteen. If you hear seven in your mind, or see the number seven in your mind (clairvoyance), or turn to the clock and see that it's 7:07, that means that the seventh exercise, Learning the Odds from the Angels, would be something powerful for you to focus on.

Remember that your intuition is attached to your higher self, that old soul inside of you that is tapped into Spirit's eternal wisdom. Your higher self can see farther down the road than your human self, and it's also privy to all the soul contracts you signed and your personal destiny here on earth. If it feels difficult to trust your intuition right now, be gentle and loving with yourself. And know that when you are trusting your intuition, you are really trusting your soul and Spirit.

If it's any consolation, trusting myself and my intuition is still something I occasionally struggle with, even as a professional psychic! Intuitives have a rule that whatever information they get about a client during a session they should just say right away. It's the reason I will often interrupt my clients when they are explaining something to me in a session. Information is coming in so quickly from the angels that I want to spit it out fast. But sometimes I will still hear that someone's child is ten or that their health issues are related to "blood sugar" and I will pause and not say this information, instead waiting for the client to confirm it first. Most of the time I will just come out with it, but when I hear in my head that the client's husband's name is Dave, and then two minutes later the client tells me their husband's name is Dave, I'm left kicking myself! We're all works in progress when it comes to trusting our intuition ... even people who make their living off of their intuition!

Instead of "talk it out," you might employ the mantra "feel it out," meaning if you have an insightful thought or hunch, pay attention to it, and then feel into it to see if you think it came from your intuition. It probably did!

Receiving Messages About Other People

Intuition Golden Rule #21: *Your spiritual guidance squad might give you information about someone in your life. You were given this information for a reason, so give yourself time to decide what action step to take.*

Hearing the name of someone in the client's life during a reading can be hugely helpful when they had not planned on talking about that person. Putting a name into my mind—or a relationship, like "brother"—is the angels' way of letting me and the client know that there is something going on with this individual or that for some reason this person needs to be discussed. An extreme example of this was when the angels gave me a name toward the end of a session with a client—and when I repeated the name to the client, he had to think a minute. The angels kept saying the name over and over in my mind, always a sign that this person needs to be discussed. "Oh, Julia is my old college buddy's wife!" he suddenly realized. I started giving him some information on this woman, who was struggling more than anyone knew. We got a few great insights from the angels that confirmed we were talking about the right woman, and my client was able to pass on some information to his friend and his wife that would be useful. I love this story because it proves that Spirit is always trying to send you messages and will work in unexpected and miraculous ways to get those messages across. Even if it's through a psychic who is meeting with your husband's old college buddy! Go figure!

This story relates to *your* intuition as well. Once you start to improve your intuition, you will receive intuitive hits about the people in your life. Then, the angels say, you have to decide with whom to share the information. You would never want to be indiscreet and gossip or hurt anyone. But the angels say that by and large you are given intuitive information about loved ones so that you can help or better understand them.

If you get a strong intuitive feeling about someone, and the matter is delicate and you are not sure how to proceed, get quiet and ask your angels what you should do with this information. You should then get some feeling or clairsentient guidance about next steps. It might be as simple as just being kinder to this person, the angels explain, if you receive intuitive information that they are going through a rough patch. If you get intuitive information that someone who hurt you felt like he was doing the right thing for your own good, it might make it easier to forgive this person. Asking the angels for insight into the true motivations of others can be quite enlightening!

The Most Important Intuitive Hits Are Often Not the Most Obvious

Intuition Golden Rule #22: *Just because an intuitive hit is dramatic does not always mean it is super helpful. Sometimes it's the subtler intuitive insights about people's motivations and blocks that are more significant.*

I regularly feel as if I am finishing my client's sentences, or that I could if I let myself. Once a client said, "My girlfriend and I are thinking of moving."

"To Paris?" I asked.

"Yes!" the client said. She and her girlfriend lived in Canada, and as it was the client's first session with me, I could never have known they were thinking of a move to France. I just heard "Paris" in my mind.

Intuiting this type of information can be important in order to confirm for the client that I really am tuned into them. But ultimately it's not that helpful. After all, the basic information—facts about your life or what you are about to say to me—you already know. It would be much more helpful to give the client some new ideas about what to do when they get to Paris or what the challenges and potential might be during their time there.

I'm much more fascinated when I can hone in on wounds that need healing, or patterns and subconscious blocks that are holding the client back. That's where the gold comes in a reading. Spirit is giving me an image of a rock with a thin but bright vein of gold running through it. That's really what the angels and I are trying to do in a reading: excavate that vein of gold that is buried in someone's life or psyche that will unlock a whole new level of potential for the them.

So just because you do not have a very "dramatic" intuitive hit—like meeting someone for the first time and intuiting their age or occupation correctly without being given any leading information—do not despair. Look for intuitive hits that have less of a wow factor but are actually more significant, like that this new friend you just met has trouble being vulnerable because of childhood issues or isn't yet in touch with the fact that they are highly sensitive. This is the real gold.

Keeping the Faith

Intuition Golden Rule #23: *Staying optimistic is like increasing the blood flow or life force to your intuition. Being positive—while still acknowledging emotions like fear and anger or challenging realities like illness or job loss—can actually increase the amount of guidance you receive from your intuition.*

I titled this section almost exactly as I heard it from the angels: "Keep the faith." What the angels meant was "remain positive and optimistic." When we are positive, it shines a light on solutions. Think of something that is troubling you like a walk through a dark, isolated wood. Optimism is that light that will illuminate your path out. I'm also getting an image of a hot pink highlighter pen and a page of dense black and white text, and am being shown that remaining positive will highlight the best options for you.

"Well, wouldn't my intuition just show me the path out of the woods" you might think, "even if I had lost all hope?" Not necessarily. Sometimes our intuition leads us and sometimes we help to lead it. The angels are giving me an image of a dog who is trained to search things out. The owner gives the dog something to sniff, perhaps a piece of clothing, and then the dog goes out to find and match that scent. The angels tell me this is the perfect metaphor for how we sometimes interact with our intuition. We can give our intuition instructions or focus, like remaining hopeful for a positive solution, and then our intuition will, like the dog, go hunt that down.

How does your intuition accomplish this? I'm getting an image of a supercomputer, and the angels tell me our intuition can plug into the "wiring" of the universe's own supercomputer. Once plugged in, our intuition can search for what we want: a romantic partner, a better way to manage a chronic health issue, a new hobby, more friends, extra income.

Our intuition will analyze all the possibilities immediately open to us in the universe to find the best fit for our desire.

The angels are also telling me that when we are positive, it actually encourages our intuition! So the more positive or hopeful you can remain about a situation, without getting attached to one specific outcome, the more fuel you pump up your intuition with to go out and find a solution, and the more options you let your intuition know you are open to.

Staying positive is not a 24/7 goal. It's important to let yourself feel sad, frustrated, and angry. But try to keep picking yourself back up again, telling yourself that somehow, some way, there is a miracle out there tailor-made just for you. Your intuition can help you find it!

Being Present to Life

Intuition Golden Rule #24: *Living in the moment is one of the best ways to increase your intuition. You will be more present and recognize more intuitive guidance that might otherwise slip through the cracks of your awareness.*

We're constantly reminded of reasons to be more present. "Live in the moment," people say. Being more present is supposed to help your mood, your relationships, your career … maybe it can even help with world peace! But did you realize that being present to life in general is crucial to developing sharp, reliable intuition? That's because intuitive cues can be very subtle.

Imagine a rock drummer banging away, doing fill after fill, symbols crashing. Sometimes your intuition will hit you over the head with guidance this way. But if intuition were musical, it would be more accurately described as similar to the single pluck of a harp string. If your ear is not trained to "hear" them, or there is too much noise in your mind or environment, you can miss intuitive cues in the hustle and bustle of today's hectic modern world. It is probably easier for people who are sensitive to pick up on intuitive guidance, because people who are sensitive naturally pick up on more, and pick up on it with less effort. That is why sensitive people like lots of quiet time—the world can prove slightly overwhelming for sensitive folks!

I'm hearing from the angels that when you are present you will start to get more intuitive guidance. The angels are showing me an image of a baseball pitcher throwing a ball to someone who is in the outfield picking daisies. What is the pitcher's motivation? Pretty soon the pitcher will realize that no one is looking for these balls and not throw them as often. Think of the pitcher as your angels or your intuition and the ball as guidance. This is why guidance will seem to speed up or become more plentiful when you pray or ask for an angel's or the universe's help in your thoughts or journal. You are sending up a smoke signal not only that you need assistance, but that your third eye is peeled.

Restorative Rest for Your Body and Nervous System

Intuition Golden Rule #25: *If you are feeling rundown, either physically, emotionally, or mentally, your intuition will be rundown too. Think of yourself and your life holistically—your intuition does not exist in a vacuum.*

Often when I am writing an article or book, the universe will send me a lesson about the subject I'm exploring. While I was working on this chapter, the angels reminded me of the importance of something quite simple yet fundamental to properly functioning intuition: getting enough rest. Just as there is a connection between body and mind, there is a connection between your body-mind and your intuition, especially your nervous system. The angels had already given me the idea to emphasize the importance of rest in this chapter, and I had set aside an evening to begin working on this section of the book, but there was one big problem: when I sat down at the computer, I realized I was exhausted!

I'd had a demanding week—way more demanding than usual, with many work and social engagements—and I was physically and intellectually pooped. I honestly could not even remember a time when I had felt more tired, as I usually take great care to plan my days so that I feel comfortable and rested. It was no coincidence that on the same evening I was more tired than I could ever recall being, I had also scheduled myself to write a section on rest! Here came the lesson, and I knew it.

When I work on a book I get so excited that I want to be chipping away at it constantly. Maybe you have a hobby or passion project or activity that brings you a similar kind of joy and purpose. So I was disappointed when my intuition told me I desperately needed a mellow night binge-watching a fun show. Yet I gave in, ordered in my favorite meal, assumed the position on the couch, and zoned out for two hours. Then the funniest thing started to happen. Once my body and mind had rested for a while, I began to receive excellent information from my intuition about what to write, even though I was not consciously thinking about the book at all. Claircognizant ideas and clairaudient messages began to float to the surface of my mind, so I jotted down notes, intending to start writing the following day after a good night's sleep. After all, I now had the whole section planned out, thanks to my intuition!

What happened when I let my body, my mind, and, most of all, my nervous system rest? The fuel gauge on my intuition slowly began to go up. That's because our bodies and minds are the "fuel" for our intuition. Everyone gets tired some days or has busy weeks when they become rundown. But if you are chronically overextending and overtaxing your body or mind, your intuition will run out of gas.

The angels say that you can always try an intuitive exercise to discern just how rundown you are.

Picture a fuel gauge like the one on the dashboard of a car. Then ask the angels how full your tank is. You could hear that it's three fourths of the way full (clairaudience), or you might be shown an image of a needle dipping below the red danger mark (clairvoyance). You might just get an intellectual understanding that you are running on empty and why (claircognizance), or you could sense through a feeling that you are slightly rundown and operating at half full (claisentience).

The angels gave me another clairvoyant image to describe how exhaustion affects intuition: a shy child hiding in the background. Your intuition will serve you in times of danger or stress, of course. But when running on "red alert" becomes something your nervous system considers default mode, or you are working such long hours that you fall in bed every night with your body aching, your intuition will hide out, like that small child in my vision, until it feels like things are safe. Your intuition is probably powerful beyond your imagination, but it is also delicate. Just like sensitive people can be both delicate and very powerful, so can your intuition.

Try to have a little time each day with low stimulation— soothing music; breaks from the internet, email, and social media; breaks from the news or upsetting conversations with colleagues and loved ones; breaks from books or movies that are violent or disturbing. This low stimulation is like petting a cat. Soon your nervous system will be purring.

ANGEL EXERCISE:
Blindfold Your Brain and Use Your Gut

This exercise is designed to get you in the habit of checking in with your intuition more often. Much like a person who is blind will begin to rely more on and develop better hearing, so will your intuition become stronger when you get in the habit of "blindfolding" your brain or the logical and analytical side of yourself. As I mentioned before, you really should consult your intellect, your emotions, and your intuition when making decisions, especially significant ones. That's why for this exercise I want you to only concentrate on small decisions: which road to take on your way home from work, which dress to wear to a party, etc.

For one week, try to make at least one small decision each day—whether to order a latte or a tea, for example—based only on your intuitive hunches. Don't make this hard on yourself, just try not to *think* your way to the answer. You might be coming home from a long day at the office, wondering which would be more relaxing: reading a great book at home or going for a long hike in nature. Even though the sun is shining and the river or woods or park near your home is calling, you hear "rest" in your mind. Once you get home and assume the position on the couch you realize how badly you needed to take a physical break. Or maybe you just spoke to a friend who lives on the other side of the country last week and everything was fine with them. Yet you keep getting the urge to check in with them again. You keep thinking, "But I just spoke to them! It will seem weird to call again." When you do call you find out they just lost their grandmother, or their job, or their girlfriend. "Hearing from you is really cheering me up," they say.

Keep a daily log in a journal each evening about what decision you made based on intuition and the outcome. Hopefully at least a few times during the week you will be pleasantly surprised by the direction your intuition steered you in. Keep in mind this intuitive information could come to you through one of the four clairs or any of the eleven magical ways that angels or your higher self send you guidance: opportunities, music, synchronicities, oracle cards, dreams, people, numbers, nudges, relationships, whispers, animals, and nature.

The following are questions to ask yourself at the end of the week in your journal. You can answer yes or no. If you answer yes, jot down details of the experience so you can remember it later. Some questions do require you to elaborate and you might receive even more intuitive hits as you think and feel through your answers.

1. Did I receive any clairaudient intuitive guidance, like a voice in my mind?

2. Did I receive any clairvoyant intuitive guidance, like a picture in my mind?

3. Did I receive any claircognizant guidance, like a download of information from heaven?

4. Did I receive any clairsentient guidance, like a feeling?

5. Did doing this exercise make my intuition seem heightened this week, like having intuitive dreams or being more sensitive to the energy of people or places?

6. Did I see any angel numbers this week?

7. Did I get a sense of a method, or methods, that my angels or higher self like to consistently use to send me guidance?

8. Did I receive intuitive guidance through animals and nature this week?

9. Did my spiritual guidance squad send me any special songs?

10. Did a person in my life give me some advice that felt very wise, significant, or like it was coming from Spirit?

11. Was there an opportunity that showed up out of the blue for me this week?

12. Was there a realization this week of why a past relationship came into my life?

13. What was the most enlightening part of this week regarding my intuition?

14. What was the most disappointing or challenging part of this week regarding my intuition?

15. Did I feel like I connected with any one specific member of my spiritual guidance squad?

16. Did I have an increase in synchronicities or meaningful coincidences?

17. How might I change the way I make decisions or use my intuition or interact with my spiritual guidance squad going forward based on my experiences and reflections this week?

18. What did I enjoy most about relying more on my intuition this week?

8

REALIZING YOUR
FULL POTENTIAL IN
INTUITION & LIFE

I LIKE TO use that phrase "highest potential" a lot. But what does it mean? Living at your highest potential means at the highest level of good for you. Many factors play into your highest potential. It was carefully woven into my fate that I did not become independently wealthy at age twenty-five, for example. My highest potential around money had a ceiling on it at that time. If I had won the lotto or come into a significant inheritance it could have interfered with my life path. I write books and do psychic readings because I love it, but part of what got me started initially was that I needed the money! (Some people who are born into or marry into great wealth might have had that as part of their soul contract so that they can accomplish significant philanthropy work, etc.) And all the writing gigs (for money) I had prior to writing books on spirituality gave me the knowledge and tools and contacts to publish books like this one. In the same vein, when I was thirty and very ill, there was a ceiling on how good my health could get at that moment in time. I had so much learning and healing to do that my highest potential for health then was drastically different than it is now at forty-three, when I have gotten my hormones balanced, regulated my thyroid, take all the vitamins and minerals I need, detoxed heavy metals, overhauled my diet, learned to love myself more, and so on. You might have a relationship in your life with a lot of water under the bridge, a relationship in which you and another person have grown in different directions. Your highest potential there might be forgiving each other and moving on. Sometimes rebuilding is not in the cards. This is often what happens in a divorce.

Your highest potential in areas of your life will change over time. Certainly earning potentials can change based on your current level of skill, the state of the economy, how much time you have to work, and shifts in your industry. Romantic potential can change based on whether you are open and looking or still healing and taking a "time out" after a big breakup. The angels are whispering that soul contracts about when and how you will meet someone who is destined to be a lover can affect the current potential too. Destiny and soul contracts can restrict or expand our highest potential. The late Louise Hay, author and founder of Hay House Publishing, obviously had a destiny where the sky was the limit as far as her career was concerned. Yes, she worked very, very hard, made the most of her opportunities, took risks, made sacrifices, and stayed true to her vision. But her highest potential, in a soul contract sense, must have been enormous, which helped her publishing company become the international powerhouse it is today. Amazingly, she did not write her first book until she was fifty-one years old, and opened her publishing company in 1988 at the age of sixty-two. Perhaps Louise's potential to be an author, entrepreneur, and public figure did not open up in her soul contract until later in life.

We are also sometimes limited by lessons we need to learn. I can reflect on times in my life and see that I was held back in what I could achieve because I needed to gather some wisdom before moving onto a bigger playing field or level of potential. You can speed this process up by asking the angels for advice on what you need to learn, master, face, or heal to change your highest potential.

This applies to your intuition as well—ask the angels what steps you can take to increase your highest potential regarding your intuitive abilities. The angels might send you signs or gut instincts about cleaning up your diet, meditating, praying, releasing your fears or expectations about your intuition, healing old wounds, expressing your emotions, spending more time in nature, forgiving yourself, or reading books or taking a course on intuition.

Much of what we will cover in this chapter will help you better achieve your highest potential by examining the things that are holding you back, many of which you are not consciously aware of.

Subconscious Blocks, Childhood Patterns, and Past Wounds

I cannot overstate the significance of subconscious blocks, which is funny because there was a time when I didn't put much stock in them. But after discovering some of my own—and how they have sabotaged me in the past—as well as having clients' subconscious blocks come up so often in sessions, I am a firm believer in rooting them out. Becoming aware of and transforming subconscious blocks is one of the most powerful ways to heal and change your life. Luckily your intuition can aid you in discovering them.

Subconscious blocks and patterns are things that are operating in your life all the time, but you are not consciously aware of them. I asked the angels to send me a metaphor to help illustrate how subconscious blocks work in our lives and they sent me a pretty gross one! The angels gave me an image of a wound, one that is bloody and filled with puss. When cleaning a wound, of course you spend time disinfecting it, draining it of any liquid, etc. But at some point if the wound does not heal naturally, you might have to rethink your approach. That might be when a doctor opens it up and finds that—aha!—there was a tiny splinter buried deep in the wound, or maybe an ingrown hair. Just a tiny, innocent splinter of wood or single hair, but look at all the damage it caused! Once the splinter or hair is removed, the wound can heal normally, when kept clean and bandaged. This is very similar to how subconscious blocks and patterns work in our lives. Sometimes we are trying to shift or heal an aspect of our lives and don't realize that a subconscious block buried very deep down is playing a huge role in our inability to shift or heal this situation.

I'll give you a concrete example from my own life. As I've mentioned, I struggled with many health issues for years. Thankfully I have been feeling great for the past six years and I'm healthier than I have ever been in my life. I was not making these past health issues up in my mind and they were not mere manifestations of mental or emotional issues. I am a firm believer in seeing doctors and other health-care professionals, and I would never tell someone suffering from a physical ailment "it's all in your head" or that the ailment is a manifestation of something spiritual or intellectual. I believe when we are sick there are many things at play, and that physical ailments need to be addressed by competent health-care professionals. That's why I would get so angry when anyone would tell me that part of my health issues were really "lack of self-love."

I was told that by several spiritual healers early on during my ten-year healing journey. Now, these healers weren't denying other physical issues, and they never advised me not to see doctors. They were just trying to alert me to the fact that lack of self-love was somewhere in the mix. I felt terrible in those early days, like I was dying or losing my mind, and I knew the most important thing was to work on my physical body with health-care professionals. I'd have to deal with fancy-schmancy subconscious blocks later!

Over the course of those ten years I kept discovering new pieces of the puzzle and handling them. These were real physical ailments that I needed real professional help for, and I am grateful for those people who helped me sort out my physical body. Because of them I'm alive and healthy, with the energy to write this book, work with clients, and have a full personal life.

But once I was toward the end of my healing journey, I looked back and realized that I had made the process much harder on myself and it had taken much longer to complete because of a lack of self-love, which, for me, stemmed from traumas in my childhood and young adult life. One of the most glaring ways I self-sabotaged my healing process was by not asking for help from friends and family. No one ever made me dinners or offered to clean my house, in part because I never asked and I never let anyone know just how sick I really felt. I did have the good sense to ask my father for help with my medical bills, help that he thankfully gave me—yet I only asked because my back was against the wall and I had no way to pay the bills on my own (I was already working full-time and was too weak to take on a second job).

My desire to try and "go it alone" with my illness, subconsciously, was a mix of not believing I deserved help (lack of self-love) and not believing I would receive it if I asked or even demanded it (again, this all goes back to childhood wounds—many of you might have similar issues). There was also a punishing quality to the way I went about my healing process, which a trusted therapist pointed out to me. I did not cut myself slack or try to nurture myself. It was almost as if the worse I felt, the harder I was on myself. It was only near the end of my healing journey that I discovered these blocks or was open to learning about them, but learning about them helped me make choices that got me all the way well.

Many subconscious blocks *do* go back to childhood. I remember that once a big change was happening in my life, but the change was positive and one I had been wanting for years. Yet I found myself in the shower one day feeling pure panic about this change! Consciously I knew transition times can be stressful for any human, but this was an extreme reaction. When one of your own emotional reactions to something feels strange or over-the-top, don't be afraid to ask your intuition if there is a subconscious issue at play. When I asked my intuition what was going on that day in the shower, I was reminded that times of big change are always especially challenging for me, because whenever a big change happened for the first nineteen years of my life, it was usually very negative. So I subconsciously equated all change with trauma.

I find that clients respond to the angels telling them, through me, that they have a subconscious block about something in one of three ways.

Let's say, for example, that I am doing a session with a client and the angels tell me the client has a subconscious block that "men can't be trusted." This block, while subconscious, might make perfect sense to the client. "Oh! Of course!" they could reply. Perhaps the client had issues with their father growing up or divorced a husband recently, and it makes sense to the client that their subconscious, as a protection mechanism, might have started sending out the signal that *no* man is trustworthy. Subconscious blocks seem to have this black and white, all or nothing tone or logic to them.

If the subconscious block is something that comes as a shock to the client, but is maybe something that seems plausible, or perhaps something they even project by accusing others of, they might react by saying, "Interesting. Okay, I never would have guessed that, but it's something to think about that makes sense."

The third way a client might react to subconscious blocks coming into a reading is by saying very firmly, "Nope, that's not me! I would never think something as extreme as 'all men can't be trusted.'" In those rare cases, I gently remind clients that this is a *sub*conscious block and something they are not aware of consciously, so it *can* come as a shock or seem outlandish.

Years ago, I uncovered a subconscious block about myself that was extremely shocking. I had decided I wanted to earn more money after making the same amount every year for many years. One day while I was cleaning the kitchen I asked the angels to tell me if I had any subconscious blocks around my finances that were preventing me from earning more money. Then, as I was wiping down a countertop, I heard these words clearly in my mind: "You're afraid to make more money than your mother." My first reaction was, "That's ridiculous!" It made no logical sense. My mother had been a single mom who worked full-time but made a very modest lower-middle class income. I was earning more than my mother had, but when I thought about it, that was mainly due to inflation, as my mother had stopped working in the early 90s just before her death. What she was making then was roughly equivalent to what I was making now if you factored in inflation. Yet why in the world would I be "afraid" or even "uncomfortable" making more money than my mother? There was no logical reason, but I quickly came up with many emotional ones.

The angels showed me an image of a race, and one runner passing another. This is a reminder that it can feel "wrong" or even "rude" to go farther or achieve more in any area of your life than your parents did. Again, this is a primal emotional reaction, and not necessarily a logical one.

It can also feel uncomfortable to live in a way that is different from how you were raised. This doesn't *just* mean that changing economic status can feel uncomfortable. In relation to the way you were raised, it can also be uncomfortable to change your views on faith or to change the city, state, or even country you live in. Growing up in a sad, angry, or generally dysfunctional household and then choosing to live as an adult in a way that is more healthy and loving can at first feel uncomfortable. Subconsciously, many people tend to repeat the patterns of their parents and their own childhoods, even the negative ones, because it feels safe and familiar.

I accepted this information from the angels and worked with this subconscious block around my mother's income by reminding myself in my thoughts that "it is safe to make more money than my mother." I came up with this mantra by consulting my intuition, and you can come up with similar mantras to address your subconscious blocks. About a year later I did begin making significantly more money. My increase in income wasn't just because of discovering this block, but I'm sure that helped!

If an intuitive or friend or anyone else tells you about a subconscious block they think you have, be open to it. Don't reject the information outright, even if it feels farfetched. Let the idea of this subconscious block sit on you for a bit. Then, if it still doesn't resonate after a few days or preferably weeks, let it go. I can be wrong and so can well-meaning family and friends! If you suspect someone has suggested you are "blocked" about something for a specific reason and you feel this person is off, go to your own intuition to find out the information. The next exercise is designed to help you do precisely that.

ANGEL EXERCISE:
Uncovering Subconscious Blocks with Archangel Gabriel

I have discovered many of my own subconscious blocks using my own intuition, and you can do the same. Talk therapy is also a marvelous tool. I've asked Archangel Gabriel to be with you as you perform this journal exercise, because Gabriel is a master at communication and this exercise helps you communicate with your subconscious mind. All you need is a journal, something to write with, and a quiet place to contemplate. Ask your higher self and Archangel Gabriel the following questions.

Once you identify a subconscious block, come up with a simple mantra to help heal that block. For example, if you discover the block, "I cannot be trusted with money," work with this mantra: "Money flows to me easily because I trust myself with money." Then follow up the mantra with action steps and be more mindful of your finances. Please know that a mantra alone will not work. If you are always overspending and never saving, a mantra will not heal this block. Changes in your behavior both in the practical world as well as psychological healing will probably be required to shift a block. Mantras can inspire us to make those changes though, or help keep us on track. And remember, shifting patterns often takes time, so be patient with yourself.

You will also need to do the harder work of discerning where this block came from or why it's there. Knowing the block came from nothing you have done, but rather was inherited from your parents' financial history, for example, is helpful. Just keep in mind that the mantra must be accompanied by changes in your attitude, awareness, and behavior.

1. What is my biggest subconscious block around romantic love? Write down the first thing that comes to mind, and explore this in your journal. The first answer

your intuition gives you to any question is often very powerful. As the week goes on you will probably have other answers to this question come to you. Return to your journal and record them. Follow these steps for each question.

2. What is my biggest subconscious block with my health?

3. What is my biggest subconscious block about my career or calling?

4. What subconscious block is holding me back the most right now?

5. What is my most significant subconscious block that stems from childhood?

6. What is one of my smaller or less dramatic subconscious blocks from childhood?

7. Which subconscious block of mine is particularly punishing or self-sabotaging?

8. Which subconscious block has deep roots and will take real work or help to change?

9. Which subconscious block of mine would be easy to heal?

10. Which subconscious block of mine, if healed, would positively transform almost every area of my life?

11. Which subconscious block of mine would come as the biggest shock to me?

12. What is my biggest subconscious block around money and abundance?

13. Which subconscious block is holding me back from loving myself more?

Embracing the Uniqueness of Your Soul

The angels want me to make this point about uniqueness here because it's something that comes up so often in readings. People have difficulty understanding the folks in their life and difficulty accepting them. The angels suggest that one of the most powerful things you can do for another soul is let them be who they are. It's also one of the most powerful things you can do for yourself. This will facilitate living at your highest potential.

One of the fascinating things about doing intuitive readings is that you meet people of "all walks of life." But what I really get in these readings is a look into someone else's soul, and every soul is unique—with a unique history, personality, and life purpose. Look around at the people in your life—the friends, family, clients, and coworkers with whom you share close relationships. Each one is unique. *Extremely* unique, the angels say. Even when I am told by the angels during a reading that certain members of a family—say a father and daughter or brother and sister—are very similar, there are still vast differences. I know it's a cliché, but the angels are reminding me of the old saying about how "no two snowflakes are exactly alike."

In recent years, scientists have weighed in on this old adage and decided that even in the very rare case where two snowflakes look similar under a microscope, they would never be the same on an atomic level. Imagine a cold, wet winter day and how many different snowflakes fall from the sky. Now imagining so many unique souls falling from the "sky," floating "down" from heaven to find a home here on earth will not seem so farfetched. As nature proves, Spirit's "capacity for creation is infinite," the angels explain.

The angels are reminding me that it's not just a soul's core personality that makes them unique, but, like the snowflake, it's all the things that happen to them over the course of this life, and past lives too. Part of what makes a snowflake unique is its journey from the sky to the ground. The other particles it picks up or attaches to along the way, as well as temperatures, wind gusts, and more, inform a snowflake's shape. The experiences that you have in this life and had in past lives maybe do not so much change but *inform* the soul.

Beyond people being made unique by their experiences in this life and past lives, they are also unique in the "blueprint" of their soul. The angels are showing me typical blueprints, like you might see an architect use when they are designing a house. When I ask how souls are made, the angels give me the words "magic" and "intricate," and they show me the image of a hand sewing a thread into a thick blanket that is made up of too many threads to count, each thread a different color and thickness and material, making up a blanket, or soul, that is incredibly beautiful, fascinating, and complex.

So now we have the life experiences, the blueprint or threads that make up the soul's core nature, and third, we have the life path or soul purpose of each individual soul. Sometimes a partner or loved one will strongly disagree with someone else's career choice, their decision to move to a new location, or even how they choose to view the world. Beyond choices that hurt ourselves or others, it can be futile and even damaging to relationships when you try to do more than simply state your reservations about a loved one's choice. Of course we want to warn a loved one when we think they are not doing something in their best interest. But sometimes people will issue ultimatums or allow relationships to become very strained because a loved one is not behaving the way they would like. Maybe giving up the 9 to 5 and 401K and moving to Bali to sell beach towels is exactly what your sister needs to do right now. It's the exact opposite of what you want out of life, but you aren't her. And keeping her "safe" may not help keep her happy or fulfill her unique life purpose and destiny. And remember, Spirit is telling me, sometimes the way people find out what they do want is by first trying things and learning what they don't want. Perhaps an adventure now is the stepping stone to something much different later. Remember that family and friends are on journeys. There are so many twists and turns in the road that we rarely foresee where they will end up. I've had several readings with clients who have a younger sibling who won't, in the client's opinion, "settle down and be responsible." Yet I have been told by the angels that when this young person gets a little older they will make a ton of money. This more adventurous and risk-taking soul may have trouble settling down in their early 20s, but will eventually do very well as a businessperson or stockbroker.

Your soul DNA, or blueprint, is made up of many different archetypes, like healer, teacher, artist, lover, nurturer, scholar, activist, etc. Usually a few of those archetypes are dominant or more pronounced. Sometimes I will read for someone with the "free spirit" archetype dominating their soul DNA, for example. Free spirits can be intense or laid-back, extroverts or introverts, artists or CEOs.

Are friends and family always on you to settle down, straighten up, and start leading a "normal" life? I tell clients with a dominant free spirit archetype to get comfortable with the fact that they might have lots of interests and passions and love to travel or move around. If you are a free spirit, celebrate and own your unconventionality! Cinema's most beloved free spirit, Maria from The Sound of Music, teaches a very rigid, sad family how to loosen up and listen to their hearts. The shadow side of this archetype is a tendency to become a little ungrounded. Like a balloon dancing in the sky, delighting those below, unless free spirits tie their string to the earth, they will fly away.

The warrior is another popular soul archetype. These folks are known as "the rock" at home, work, or among their friends. They possess incredible discipline and drive, can accomplish a ton, and are often given challenges from the universe to display their strength and resilience. The shadow side of this archetype is that often warriors tend to go it alone, either forgetting to ask for help or having a fear of showing vulnerability. They can likewise have a problem knowing when to cry uncle and say, "That's all I can take!"

If you have issues with the way a family member or close friend is navigating their life, ask yourself, "Is this something their soul needs to do?" Then get quiet and listen not even to your angels this time, but to your heart. Your heart has its own wisdom and so many answers for you, if you will take the time to connect with your heart and listen. Sometimes answers from the heart can be inconvenient or even painful, but they resonate with a truth that is undeniable.

Past Lives Reveal Our Roots

Past lives do not always come up in my sessions with clients, although the angels will shed light onto a client's past lives if it is significantly affecting them today. Receiving information about who we were in previous incarnations can explain some of our patterns and coping mechanisms in this life. A past life might be the reason why you are drawn to a certain culture; why you had a strong calling to be a healer, artist, mother, scientist, inventor, entertainer, builder, or entrepreneur even as a child; or why you have certain phobias or blocks. Past lives can especially help to explain some of our most intimate relationships with people in this life.

The angels, and particularly Archangel Gabriel, have told me that not all but many of the people in our lives today have been in previous incarnations with us. Think of it like a theater troupe of actors that continuously puts on plays out of the same venue (earth). Every season the play changes, the characters are different, and the props are new. Yet behind the masks, playing the roles are the same souls, the same personalities. This is not always true, as sometimes souls who are not a part of your typical troupe or soul family will make a promise to meet up and play starring roles in your life on a debut run together. Maybe we could think of this as a "limited engagement."

If the idea of past lives does not resonate with you or your spiritual beliefs, I completely respect that. The concept resonates deeply with me because it has always sounded plausible and been fascinating to me, and because I've had so many experiences with clients, as well as my own personal experiences, where examining possible past lives has greatly improved or explained this life. In an effort to maintain the confidentiality and anonymity of my clients, I will share some of my own past lives, as told to me by the angels.

When I wrote *Angel Insights*, I wanted very much to come out of the closet and let people know that I spoke to angels. Naturally, clients, close friends, and family members were already aware of this fact. Yet when you put something out to the general public, it's a different level of exposure. I was never afraid of being thought of as "kooky" or "wrong." What bothered me was a fear of being persecuted.

Some spiritual traditions, or the people who represent them, don't always look kindly on a person saying they can hear an angel's voice or see a vision given to them by Spirit. Joan of Arc was burned at the stake for saying she could speak to Archangel Michael, after all. And in my US homeland we have a sad history of persecuting people for their spiritual beliefs, like the men and women who were burned at the stake in New England in the 1600s because they were accused of being Wiccans, a Pagan religion that simply worships, honors, and utilizes this earth and it's powerful, positive energies. More recently, the US experienced a rise in hate crimes against many groups, including Jews and Muslims.

Yet I knew my extreme fear of persecution around coming out publicly as an intuitive was out of line with the reality of any pushback I could expect. Of course I would receive some, but there are many famous psychics who have helped to mainstream and normalize this craft. After ruling out a subconscious block, I realized that the over-the-top fear I was experiencing let me know a past life wound or trauma might be in play.

You may have an unnatural fear of poverty, which could be traced to a past life when you were malnourished or experienced significant want. Perhaps you experienced a grueling, painful childbirth in a past life, and despite being healthy and surrounded by top-notch medical professionals in this life, you are now terrified to get pregnant. You could have a pronounced fear of sexual intimacy, which might be traced back to taking holy orders in a past life, your lack of sexual experience or a stigma around sexuality in a past life, or a sexual trauma experienced in a past life.

Was I ever burned at the stake for my spiritual beliefs? Not necessarily. Although the angels showed me clearly in a vision that I was a monk sometime during the 1500 to 1600s, working alone in a cell on an illuminated manuscript. This helped explain why one of my favorite things to do is sit alone in a room for hours and write, a great example of how past lives can give us clues to our soul's unique personality and predilections. This vision of me as a monk five hundred years ago also helped explain why I might have such a disproportionate fear about coming out as a psychic in a book during this century. I had probably rightly lived in fear of going against my church in the years I was a monk, and had surely seen people mercilessly punished for doing so. Once I discerned that my fear was based in a past-life experience, the fear did not magically dissipate; however, that knowledge did give me the courage to face my fear and write the book anyway. Some fears are meant to be heeded and some are meant to be only acknowledged. Each one of us has a unique path, journey, destiny. All we can do is be true to our own, lifetime after lifetime.

Past lives can also shed light onto our romantic choices. Fairly often I will have a client say something like, "I met this person, and we had such a strong instant attraction. I have never felt anything like this before in my life." The sparks! The energy! The intensity! The sexual chemistry!

There can be a magnetic pull toward this person that is hard to explain or understand logically. It's a feeling that is undeniable, though. Many people will get into fairy tale territory here, and think, "This is meant to be! This is my ultimate soul mate!"

This feeling is usually, in my opinion, only proof of one thing—a strong past-life connection. Where humans can get tripped up is believing that just because we have a past life connection or had a past life romance with someone, that means this person has to be our "soul mate" in this life. The angels tell me that many of those "ones who got away," the people or relationships we romanticize all out of proportion, are past life romances—and many of them would never have worked in this life. The truth of the matter is, sometimes a past life relationship can result in a loving, successful, long-term, "meant to be" partnership in this life. Other times it can be a disaster. And of course these relationships can also be anything in between those two extremes—like a way to work through or release past life issues or teach each other some soul lessons. All that electric, Romeo/Juliet, uncanny, hard-to-describe vibe should tell you is, "I have a soul connection to this person and possibly we were romantically or intimately involved in a past life or lives."

Bear in mind that if your past life connection to this person was romantic, it might have worked out in that past life about as successfully as it did for Romeo and Juliet! And know that you might not even have been lovers in a past life—you might have been soldiers on opposite sides of a war who met on the battlefield and fatally wounded each other. The angels say to be warned, because sometimes it's a case of not making the same mistake twice, or not being destined as lovers in this life because other partners would serve your happiness and growth more this time around. While past life or soul connections should be acknowledged, I advise you to base any romantic relationships in this life solely on how compatible you are right now. I also believe that when we talk about soul mates, we are talking about not just one but many soul mates we have in a lifetime, including potential romantic partners, business partners, friends, and family members.

"I don't want this person in my life next time around," clients will sometimes say to me. This might be a boss, an ex-husband, a parent, someone you were in a long, drawn-out lawsuit with, and so on. The angels' advice? "Release them with love." If you can end your relationship with this person in your current life and then either maintain a neutral energy toward them or wish them well, I think it's very helpful for severing the bond that might have kept you tethered lifetime after lifetime. There is a line in the 2017 film *Star Wars: The Last Jedi* that describes this concept perfectly. Luke tells his nephew, who wants to kill him, "Strike me down in anger and I will always be with you." Yet releasing someone with love or a neutral energy first means working through your challenging and painful emotions around this person. This approach also works with negative patterns we want to shift and release. Instead of getting angry at yourself or the pattern, try to release with love or at least neutrality.

Past Life Discernment Tools

There are many ways you might get clues to possible past lives you have lived. Here are some helpful methods:

1. **Dreams:** I once had a dream about a close friend in my current life whom I suspected I'd had a past life with. In the dream, this person and I were young girls standing on an ocean shore. In the dream, I knew the ocean was this earthly dimension. We were holding hands and debating whether to jump in. One of us was hesitant because we had both experienced difficulties in past lives, but then the other one said, "It will be fun! Remember the adventure of it all?" When I woke, the angels said it was a memory from when our souls decided to incarnate together in this lifetime.

2. **Guided meditations:** At a workshop, I was once led into a general guided meditation where I began to have a past life flashback. In my past life, a current life loved one and I were siblings in Ireland in the 1800s. We were starving, as many in Ireland were at the time, and slept in a barn. The most fascinating part of my vision is that the person in my current life whom I saw sleeping in a barn in our past life together was, in this lifetime,

raised on a farm. As a child this person would often sneak out into the barn to sleep next to the animals at night. I called this person after my past life vision to say hello, though I mentioned nothing about my experience in the guided meditation. "What are you doing?" I asked casually. "Oh, going to pick up some hay," she answered. I had never had this person mention hay to me before, yet that was what we had both been eating and sleeping on in my past life memory.

3. **Answers from your spiritual guidance squad:** I once asked my spiritual guidance squad who in my life was in my soul family and had been with me in other lifetimes. "But tell me someone who would shock me," I added. I heard the name and saw the face of someone I was related to only by a marriage in my family.

4. **Your natural talents:** Are you a natural-born leader? I once saw sports highlights on the news, and the camera held for a moment on the face of a college football coach during a national playoff game. I immediately was given the information claircognizantly that this man had been a general of an army in a past life, and I could almost see his face changing and a military uniform taking shape.

5. **Archetypes:** Past life visions may not always be literal. The angels or your higher self might give you clues to a past life by showing you the clairvoyant image of an archetype. A figure the angels show me often in

meditation about myself is a warrior or solider, dressed in armor like a knight and carrying a large sword. This says more about me having a strong warrior or knight archetype to my soul than about me having been specifically a knight in a past life.

6. **Visions:** At a shaman bonfire I once saw a vision of young male Native American warriors wearing traditional dress and face paint sitting around the flames, although the people who were actually surrounding me were mostly middle aged and wearing modern, casual clothes! I felt a kinship to these warriors, like I had been one of them. I then asked the angels what I was like in that Native American lifetime, and the answer I heard was "fearless."

7. **People, places, and things:** I was once in premeditation before a session with a new client when I asked Spirit for the names of my client's guardian angels. I was given all traditional Scandinavian names. When I got on the phone with the client, I asked if she had Scandinavian heritage. "Not at all," she said, "but I am fascinated by that part of the world. I read about Scandinavian history often and I have traveled there several times." The angels told us she'd also experienced past lives in this part of the world. In the same way you can be drawn to places, periods in history, or certain activities that hold past life clues, you might be drawn to a particular friend, lover, or mentor.

If the idea of past lives does not resonate with you or match your spiritual beliefs, simply take any past life guidance from your angels as a metaphor for this life. If you see yourself on stage as a performer in the 1960s, interpret this vision as a message from your angels that you have a strong performer archetype in your soul that might be itching to get out and play!

Angel Exercise:
Discover Clues to Past Life Incarnations with Archangel Jeremiel

I'd be shocked if after all this talk of past lives you weren't curious about your own! Maybe you've already read books on past life theory, done guided meditation to see scenes from your past lives, or you might have even had a session with a psychic and asked them about your past lives. The angels, along with your higher self, will sometimes send you clues about a past life experience you had, especially when that past life can help you make sense of and heal relationships and patterns in this life.

Archangel Jeremiel helped me come up with this fun past life quiz. Archangel Jeremiel specializes in "life reviews," or helping us make sense of the past and present so we can better shape, co-create, or navigate the future. He occasionally comes into sessions with my clients when they are wanting to proactively make big changes in different areas of their lives, or when clients are starting a "new chapter" of their lives. Use the questions below as prompts to explore in your mind or your journal. Archangel Jeremiel says that if anything comes up for you in this quiz that you would like to keep exploring, just take out your journal, write him a short note, and he will try to help send you more clues about past lives as signs, synchronicities, gut instincts, aha ideas, and dreams.

1. Have you ever had a dream that you were living in a different time or culture? Pay attention to your surroundings (clothes, scenery) in these dreams. Sometimes dreams can contain clues to past lives.

2. Do you feel drawn to a certain country or culture or time period? Having extreme pride or interest in a certain part of your heritage can also be a clue to a past life.

3. Jeremiel asks, "Have you ever traveled to a place that felt like home?" This could be another part of the state you live in, a certain "type" of place (like a farm, a major city, a seaside community), or another country. Where feels like home to you?

4. Jeremiel adds that sometimes an "environment" will feel like home—a restaurant, office, or healing center. You might feel at home at work because you shared a past life with a coworker, or maybe you feel at home in a hospital or college because you were a healer or teacher in a past life.

5. "Situations" or "roles" can also feel like home—and not always in a good way! What if you were a slave or an underprivileged, undervalued person in a past life? You might be comfortable putting up with situations in this life—whether at home or work—that are not healthy or for your highest good.

6. What are you naturally good at? Archangel Jeremiel says this is an important question, as the answer has something to do with your calling or destiny. What have you always had a passion for? I have a friend who has been an artist, and getting paid for his art, since he was nine years old! He insisted that his parents take him to publications and galleries at age nine, so he could sell his art. Similarly, Leonardo DiCaprio said he begged his parents to take him on acting auditions when he was still a child. Sometimes we come into this life with a very fixed, strong path that is related to who we were in the past, and who we are on a soul level.

7. What are you afraid of? Do you have some strong phobias, like an intense fear of heights, sharp objects, the ocean, or riding on a train? Jeremiel says any fear that seems unnatural, out of balance, or over-the-top, and cannot be explained by a trauma in this life, might offer clues to a past life.

8. What do you feel at home doing? Does cooking, riding a horse, sailing, knitting, throwing pottery, nursing a

baby, gardening, or any other activity make you feel grounded, happy, and safe? Archangel Jeremiel says this could be because that activity calls forth your soul, which can make you feel relaxed and grounded. Perhaps it calls forth your soul because it is an activity or sensation you have enjoyed in many lifetimes.

9. Are there certain seasons that call to you? I have never liked summer, but love winter. And those Irish roots (in both this life and past lives) also make me very partial to gray, overcast days when the sun has been replaced by dewy mist.

10. Who are the people closest to you in your life? It's likely that these people shared some past incarnation with you. Jeremiel also says to look at people who were "pivotal" in your life, people who helped, inspired, or challenged you, like mentors, doctors, teachers, bosses, business partners, or ex-lovers. He also says that sometimes people who "trigger" us were sent for a reason—and possibly from a past life!

11. Have you ever felt an instant connection with someone? Maybe sexual sparks flew, you found yourself incredibly comfortable with someone instantly, or you had an uncanny amount in common. Jeremiel says we are often just "drawn" to people from a past life … for better or worse! But think of this phenomenon as someone approaching you in a ballroom and asking you to dance—you don't have to say yes!

12. Has someone ever appeared in your life just when
    you needed them? I have had teachers, doctors, fellow
    authors and psychics, good friends, business contacts,
    and more appear in my life just when I needed their
    influence or assistance or support. This certainly sig-
    nals a soul contract between you and this person to be
    part of each other's lives, but it might also signal a past
    life connection.

13. Do you have any historical fantasies? Maybe you pic-
    ture yourself as an ancient druid wandering in the hilly
    Welsh countryside; at a loud, colorful Egyptian bazaar
    one thousand years ago; employed as a scholar in the
    Ming Dynasty; in Paris or Moscow during their politi-
    cal revolutions; or chilling at Woodstock watching Jimi
    Hendrix, Janis Joplin, and The Who kill it on stage (or
    maybe you were at Woodstock in *this* lifetime).

14. What archetypes appeal to you? I have fantasies about
    being on stage or performing, and always have since I
    was a child, which is probably why I like appearing on
    radio shows, making videos for my YouTube channel,
    and talking to groups (and singing karaoke). Does the
    student/teacher archetype call to you? How about the
    mystic, artist, warrior, free spirit, leader, healer, nur-
    turer, scientist, philosopher, mother, father, inventor,
    athlete, builder, dreamer, pioneer, or activist? These
    archetypes might represent roles you played in past

lives. If you don't believe in past lives, these archetypes could give you some clues about the personality of your soul.

15. Are there members of your family you have a very intense relationship with? It could be intensely close or intensely challenging. Either one can signal a past life connection, which can be intense.

16. Have you ever experienced déjà vu? Met someone and felt like you'd already met them before?

17. Sit in quiet meditation with your eyes closed for at least ten minutes by first making this request: Archangel Jeremiel, please show me images that will reveal some of my possible past lives. After the meditation, record and explore any insights in your journal.

Work with the information in this chapter: accepting yourself and others, uncovering subconscious blocks, and investigating past lives. Emphasizing self-love can have a phenomenal effect on your life. If you have trouble with self-love, ask the angels to work on this issue with you!

Remember, living at your highest potential doesn't mean being perfect or having a life that appears perfect to others on social media. Living at your highest potential has much more to do with how your life *feels* than how it looks. It's about you feeling content, peaceful, engaged, happy, challenged, curious, alive, magical, confident, present, powerful, supported, and whole.

Conclusion

"WHAT DID YOU know that you could not have known?" This is the question my husband often asks me when I hang up the phone and come out of my study after a session with a client. I keep all sessions confidential, but I might reply that I intuited the client's age, the city they live in, their health condition, or their brother's name.

But what about the things I get "wrong"? Some people come to a psychic expecting them to intuit every cold hard fact of their lives, and everything that will happen to them in the future. After reading this book, I know you are much wiser than that!

Do not approach your *own* intuition in a right and wrong, black and white, rigid and unforgiving manner. This attitude will shut down a psychic's intuition, and it will also shut down yours. It's the same kind of black and white thinking that can shut down your relationship to Spirit. Intuition and Spirit are much more complex and nuanced than that.

As you play with the information and exercises in this book, your intuition will flourish. Check out the Recommended Reading section for more resources. Be gentle and patient with yourself as you take steps to improve and trust your intuition. It's a lifetime's work—work that can be frustrating at moments, but also fun and extremely rewarding! I would remind you that with intuition, practice makes perfect, but we wise souls are not aiming for unattainable perfection. The most we can hope to attain with our intuition or anything else is mastery and self-awareness that leads to more self-love.

Recommended Reading

Aron, Dr. Elaine N. *The Highly Sensitive Person: How to Thrive When the World Overwhelms You*. New York: Broadway Books, 1997.

Bodine, Echo. *The Gift: Understand and Develop Your Psychic Abilities*. Novato, CA: New World Library, 2003.

Choquette, Sonia. *Ask Your Guides: Connecting to Your Divine Support System*. Carlsbad, CA: Hay House, 2007.

———. *Diary of a Psychic: Shattering the Myths*. Carlsbad, CA: Hay House, 2003.

Dyer, Dr. Wayne. *Getting in the Gap: Making Conscious Contact with God Through Meditation*. Carlsbad, CA. Hay House, 2014.

———. *The Power of Intention: Learning to Co-Create Your World Your Way*. Carlsbad, CA: Hay House, 2005.

Gilbert, Elizabeth. *Big Magic: Creative Living Beyond Fear*. New York: Riverhead Books, 2016.

Loewe, Emma, and Lindsay Kellner. *The Spirit Almanac: A Modern Guide To Ancient Self-Care*. New York: TarcherPerigee, 2018.

Lynch, David. *Catching the Big Fish: Meditation, Consciousness, and Creativity*. New York: TarcherPerigee, 2016.

Ohotto, Robert. *Transforming Fate into Destiny: A New Dialogue with Your Soul*. Carlsbad, CA: Hay House, 2008.

Richardson, Cheryl. *The Unmistakable Touch of Grace: How to Recognize and Respond to the Spiritual Signposts in Your Life*. New York: Free Press, 2006.

Richardson, Tanya Carroll. *Angel Insights: Inspiring Messages From and Ways to Connect With Your Spiritual Guardians*. Woodbury, MN: Llewellyn, 2016.

———. *Forever in My Heart: A Grief Journal*. Berkeley, CA: Ulysses Press, 2016.

———. *Zen Teen: 40 Ways to Stay Calm When Life Gets Stressful*. New York: Seal Press/Hachette, 2018.

Sasson, Gahl. *A Wish Can Change Your Life: How to Use the Ancient Wisdom of Kabbalah to Make Your Dreams Come True*. New York: Touchstone, 2003.

Sherman, Paulette Kouffman. *The Book of Sacred Baths: 52 Bathing Rituals to Revitalize Your Spirit*. Woodbury, MN: Llewellyn, 2016.

TANYA CARROLL RICHARDSON

ANGEL
INSIGHTS

Inspiring Messages From
and Ways to Connect With
Your Spiritual Guardians

Angel Insights
Inspiring Messages From and Ways to Connect With Your Spiritual Guardians
Tanya Carroll Richardson

Angels are always with you—but who are they, and how can we communicate with them? In what ways can angels help us, and what are their limitations? Can we invite angels to play a larger role in our lives?

Angel Insights provides the fascinating, life-changing answers to these questions, and teaches you how to cultivate dynamic relationships with your guardian angels, helper angels, and archangels. Join author and intuitive Tanya Carroll Richardson as she shares messages given to her straight from the angel realm on spiritual topics like fate, free will, soul contracts, divine timing, and living as a human angel. Discover how to hone your intuition, use the power of prayer, and work with the book's angel exercises to receive divine assistance with: love • relationships • healing • protection • trauma • challenges • celebrations • joy • life purpose • self-care • being of service • the environment • grief • forgiveness • boundaries • energy clearing • change • personal growth • your sixth sense • connection to Spirit

Understanding and communicating with angels is possible for everyone. Learn to utilize the angel realm's power, wisdom, and grace to live at your full potential.

978-0-7387-4795-8, 288 pp., 5 ¼ x 8   **$15.99**

CHANTEL LYSETTE

ANGELIC

PATHWAYS

An Angel Medium's
Guide to Navigating
Our Human Experience

Angelic Pathways

An Angel Medium's Guide to Navigating
Our Human Experience

CHANTEL LYSETTE

Angelic Pathways takes an in-depth look at the relationship between humans and the benevolent hosts of heaven—the archangels.

From pre-life planning to birth to the moment a soul returns to heaven, archangels walk with humanitys every step of the way. They are our older siblings in spirit—heavenly guardians entrusted to teach and to guide. But first and foremost, they are ambassadors of the cosmos who are charged with the task of helping each human fulfill his or her divine purpose.

Through personal anecdotes and client accounts, angel intuitive Chantel Lysette shows you how to embrace the archangels for guidance and friendship, find peace in day-to-day living, and understand your purpose for this lifetime.

978-0-7387-3496-5, 264 pp., 5 ³⁄₁₆ x 8   **$15.99**

ANGEL MESSAGES

MESSAGES

Inspirational Notes
from Loved Ones

MAUDY FOWLER
AND GAIL HUNT

Angel Messages
Inspirational Notes from Loved Ones
Maudy Fowler
Gail Hunt

Your loved ones in heaven are with you all the time.

In *Angel Messages*, Maudy Fowler and Gail Hunt confirm what many people intuitively feel—angels share messages from our loved ones and they help us when we need them most. Feel the arms of the angels embrace you as you focus on the love, light, and laughter that come when you open up to these profound messages. Discover how to hear the angels as they provide guiding signs, and experience the peace and comfort of tapping into your own spiritual connection. Sharing beautiful stories and warmhearted messages, this book helps you feel the love that can only come from that special place that's beyond this world.

978-0-7387-5030-9, 216 pp., 5 ¼ x 8   **$15.99**

the
INTUITIVE
DANCE

BUILDING, PROTECTING &
CLEARING YOUR ENERGY

Atherton Drenth

The Intuitive Dance
Building, Protecting, and Clearing Your Energy
Atherton Drenth

Stop letting the negative voice in your mind create stress and instead start moving toward peace and harmony. Using practical exercises and easy-to-follow techniques, *The Intuitive Dance* helps you dance with your ego to find inner calm.

Learn how to improve your wellness and happiness as you progress through this book's three main sections: building, protecting, and clearing your energy. Along the way you'll discover how to determine your intuitive type, center and ground your energy, and rest fully when you sleep. Explore ways to cut energy cords with negative influences around you, make your living spaces more peaceful, and fill your life with abundance. By changing your inner dialogue and the harmful beliefs that may have been ingrained in childhood, you can live the truth of who you really are.

978-0-7387-4798-9, 288 pp., 6 x 9   **$16.99**

CYNDI DALE

the

SPIRITUAL
POWER

of

empathy

Develop Your Intuitive Gifts
for Compassionate Connection

The Spiritual Power of Empathy
Develop Your Intuitive Gifts for
Compassionate Connection
Cyndi Dale

Discover your innate empathic abilities with popular author Cyndi Dale as your guide. With this hands-on training course, you'll learn how to comfortably use empathy for better relationships and healing the self and others.

The Spiritual Power of Empathy presents this often-unrecognized ability in accessible ways, allowing you to discover an expanded awareness of what empathy is, how it works, and the myriad ways it manifests. Develop deeper connections with your loved ones, use specialized techniques for screening and filtering information, and gain insights on how to overcome the difficulties empaths often face. With the power of empathy, you'll transform the way you live and connect with the world around you.

2015 IPPY Award Gold Medal Winner in New Age
(Mind-Body-Spirit)

978-0-7387-3799-7, 264 pp., 6 x 9 **$16.99**